THREE YEARS
OF TUESDAY MORNINGS
156 e-mails about business and life

Steve Fales

Published by
Praeter Advisory

(p.

Three Years Of Tuesday Mornings: 156 e-mails about business and life

© 2014 by Steve Fales

Published by Praeter Advisory, Florida

Edited by Alan Williamson and Debbie Ward

Cover Design by Melissa Wolowicz

Interior Layout Design by Melissa Wolowicz

Printed in the United States of America

978-1-7331446-1-2

To Lauren and April.

Contents

Acknowledgments

One of the themes that shows up on the following pages is teamwork. That concept, in fact, had a lot to do with this book becoming a reality. Although my name appears on the cover, there are a lot of people whose efforts have been invaluable.

Many thanks to ...

- Tonya and Alan, top notch Executive Assistant and Senior Copywriter, who took hundreds of pages of raw content and turned it into something resembling a first draft.
- Melissa, the talented Graphic Designer responsible for the cover and interior page layouts, while enduring the greater challenge of my many revisions.
- Ann, extremely efficient Production Manager. She beat every deadline, because she understands me that well.
- Debbie, for being so detail oriented that even I trust her to make final edits.
- And all the people of AdServices Inc. It's been debated whether a tree falling in the woods with no living creatures around makes any noise. Without you there would not have been a reason or a venue for any Tuesday Morning E-mails.

With sincere appreciation,

Steve Fales

Introduction

In 2005 I began a practice that continues to this day. Every Tuesday morning I send an e-mail to all the employees of the advertising agency I founded many years before. It's called, simply enough, the Tuesday Morning E-Mail.

At times the TMEM, as it's also known, just informs the staff of something happening in the company. But quite often it contains what I'd like to think are insights and nuggets that enhance the readers' lives. And it's certainly not all business. Employees are whole human beings, so personal development topics receive attention as well.

After several years of TMEMs, there exists a full library of brief writings covering diverse subjects of individual and professional growth. I find myself referring to them often during conversations with friends, family, colleagues – even strangers. In the midst of a discussion I'll say, "I wrote an e-mail about that. Here's what it says."

It occurred to me that a broader audience might find these essays helpful. Thus this book, presenting three years' worth of the encouragement, inspiration, and practical advice that a group of ad agency personnel might have received in their e-mail Inboxes weekly.

Every Tuesday Morning E-Mail begins with the words "Good Tuesday Morning." More significantly they end with "Expecting great things" above my signature. And that is my hope for you. May your life, career, or organization find new levels of fulfillment as a result of reading the following pages.

Expecting great things,

Steve Fales

2014

The Two Hardest Parts – Number One

There are two parts of any task or project that are the hardest of all. One of them is – Starting It. (To find out what the other one is, see the last entry in this book.) Starting a project requires a mix of courage, vision, and willpower.

It can be scary to embark upon a new undertaking. There are so many unknowns. I might face the embarrassment of not being able to accomplish the objective. I may fail miserably, disappointing myself and others. I could even be successful and find myself in completely new territory – what's it like out there? These and many other fears flood the mind. Fortunately, there are ways to overcome each of them.

Considering the worst case scenario often helps. If we think it through, we find that usually the consequences to coming up short aren't that bad, and can certainly be resolved. As Winston Churchill said, "Failure is not fatal: it is the courage to continue that counts."

Indeed, falling short of a goal is no fun. Not taking the chance at all, however, can be even more of a downer. The deepest regrets stem from never having tackled a possible opportunity. And fear of success is very real, but the rewards of a goal accomplished far outweigh the potential negatives.

Vision plays a huge role as well. Without a clear vision of a positive outcome, there is little motivation to attempt something new. Planting a garden on a hot, humid day is not appealing in itself to most people. But thinking of the wonderful, delicious vegetables that will come in a few months, the joy of working the soil as a family, and the pride of creating something out of nothing can be enough to get us off the sofa and into the back yard.

The old saying goes "The hardest part of learning to play the violin is opening the case." Once we find the courage and have the vision, simple determination comes to bear. Get started.

The Bliss Of Boredom

The thirteen-year old sat slouched on the sofa. His posture and the look on his long face made it clear that, in his mind, all was not right with the world. "What's wrong, Honey?" his mother asked. The answer came slowly, but the message was clear: "I'm bored."

There are seasons in life when boredom seems worse than the plague. But many have learned that being bored can be a wonderful gift.

Anyone who spends much time on commercial airlines knows that a boring day of travel is actually euphoric. Much better to leave according to schedule and sleep on the flight than to navigate a maze of delays, missed connections and cancellations, or experience the excitement of severe turbulence. The latter are anything but boring, and anything but fun.

Scrambling to re-do a project on deadline that contained an error the first time will get the adrenaline pumping. Going into crisis mode to mend a relationship ramps up the energy. And hearing the doctor say "We need to talk" will stimulate the senses. In each case, however, most people would choose boredom.

When nothing is going on that sends our blood pressure spiking, it can mean that things are running smoothly. Business may not be such that a new yacht purchase is on the horizon, but orders are coming in, the bills are paid and there are reserves in the bank. It might not be family trip around the world time, but spouses are getting along, the kids are healthy, and nobody's running from the law. Does that sound boring? Maybe ... but in a good way.

The teenager's mom thought for a moment. She could point out all the options that her son had at his disposal for activities to keep himself amused. Perhaps he should be reminded that it was a beautiful day outside. Instead, she remained silent. "One day he'll only wish he could be bored" she thought, and went back to housework.

The Power Of Mindset

Mindset, or the thinking and perspective brought to a situation, has a dramatic effect on how a person reacts. Read the quick story below, and see if you relate.

Bob and Tina dated for a couple years before they were married a decade ago. They get along well despite their differences and idiosyncrasies. Bob, you see, is very disciplined and likes to have all his ducks in a row. Tina on the other hand, kind of flies by the seat of her pants. And once in awhile that causes friction.

Take a couple weeks back when Bob and Tina agreed to meet at a certain time at a coffee shop. Tina had to make a stop along the way, but she assured Bob she'd be on time. Bob was early of course.

When the hour came for Tina to arrive and she wasn't there, Bob just chuckled. "Ha, that's my wife." But ten minutes passed, and no Tina. He started to get a little irritated so he decided to call her cell phone. The call went to voice mail. "Why do we even pay for her cell phone when she often doesn't answer?", Bob thought, as he felt himself becoming annoyed.

Just then Bob's phone rang. The voice on the other end was a police officer. "Your wife has been in an accident," the voice said.

Immediately everything in Bob's mind changed. The irritations disappeared, replaced with concern for Tina. "Where is she? Is she okay? Can I come see her?" he wondered.

Bob underwent a mindset change. What seemed important a moment earlier suddenly didn't matter at all. And things he hadn't even thought of before became critical. That's how powerful mindset is.

Check your mindset about life, business, friends, family, etc. Are there attitudes that color the way you look at the world even before considering all the factors? How would your outlook be different if your mindset changed? Maybe it's worth the effort.

(By the way, Tina was okay.)

Zero Sum vs. Abundance Thinking

Is life a zero sum game, or are there enough resources to go around? The way a person answers that question will dictate a great deal about how he or she lives.

Zero sum is the belief that there are a limited number of chips on the table and that's all there ever will be. The more I have, the fewer you have, and vice versa. There can be only one winner. The pie is just so big, and if your piece increases, mine will get smaller. When philosophers, business gurus, economists, etc. speak of a situation as a zero sum game, they mean that the total of Side A's score plus Side B's score, subtracted from the total points available will always equal zero.

The opposite mindset, abundance thinking, believes that there is always enough to go around. It says that we'll put our heads together and find or create or generate more chips. The whole is greater than the sum of its parts. We each get a higher perspective by occasionally standing on each other's shoulders. By working together, we make the pie bigger, so our piece of the pie – no matter what percent of the pie that piece is – is greater than it would have been if we had not worked together.

Most often, a zero sum mentality leads to stressful, bleak environments in which people do little to foster teamwork and mutual success. Thinking in terms of abundance, on the other hand, creates alliances and teams that help everyone involved and keep organizations moving forward. The latter, no doubt, is much better.

Zero Sum vs. Abundance In An Organization

Zero sum is a belief system that leads to competitive environments in which people think that the only way they can have more is by making sure others have less. On the flip side, abundance thinking says that by working together all parties benefit. These diverse mindsets not only affect individuals but entire organizations.

In a zero sum workplace a person may think "If I admit that the other person's idea is better, that means my idea must be not be as good." This can lead to undermining the superior direction. If a mistake is made, the zero sum response will often be to conjure reasons and make excuses as to why I wasn't really at fault, but how the shortcoming was actually someone else's doing. Such office politics stifle progress and lead to suspicions on every level.

The abundance-thinking staff says "Thank you for your input. I see how your ideas, coupled with some of mine, will lead to a better conclusion that will benefit the project, accomplish the goal more effectively, and lead to a stronger team." Or, "I made a mistake here. Let's put our heads together and devise a procedure that will keep this from happening again."

An individual working in a vacuum, afraid to expose his or her weaknesses, is limited in talent and capacity. Those working in concert, however, find themselves reaching new heights. The view is far superior up there.

What Do You Think?

People live, to a great degree, in accordance with the way they think about themselves. They say things like, "I'm just no good at such and such," and it becomes truth. This principle works in a more positive way as well. The man or woman who believes that he or she has a good sense of humor is very often the life of the party.

Our vision of ourselves, therefore, determines our direction.

Napoleon Hill was a reporter who was asked to interview the wealthiest man in the world at the time, Andrew Carnegie from U.S. Steel. During the interview, Mr. Carnegie turned the tables on Napoleon Hill by commissioning him to do a study of the 500 most successful people on Earth. Andrew Carnegie provided personal introductions and asked Hill to interview them and report his findings. At the end of his study this was Napoleon Hill's conclusion: "We become what we think about."

The wisest man who ever lived was Solomon, an ancient king of Israel. God told Solomon that he could have anything he wanted, and Solomon asked for wisdom. Imagine, wisdom received directly from the hand of God. And toward the end of his life, here are some words written by Solomon: "As a man thinks in his heart so is he."

And consider this quote by Henry Ford: "If you think you can, or if you think you can't, you're right."

Henry Ford, Napoleon Hill, and wise King Solomon all understood the same truth – that how we perceive ourselves determines how we live. Get in touch with who you really are, because the vision that you have of yourself is right now determining your direction.

Possible Impossibilities

Two men sat looking up into the sky. One said, "It's wonderful that we can send people to explore the Moon and communicate all over the world by bouncing sound waves off large devices that orbit Earth." His friend replied, "You are insane! Such feats are impossible!" The year was 1600, and those feats WERE impossible ... or were they?

Is it possible for someone who's just started walking for exercise to run a marathon? Can a person who only yesterday enrolled in college obtain a Ph.D.? A man and woman have begun getting to know each other ... is a life of love and companionship possible? The answers are no – and yes.

Accomplishments that are totally unlikely today become reality when time and the right types of effort are applied to them. It takes steady progress, dedication, and a large dose of vision, but the end will ultimately be in sight. Goals broken down into next steps which are planned, prioritized, and then executed are eventually achieved.

What appears impossible may just be an idea that's ahead of its time, or that is outside the grasp of current experience. It starts by doing what we can today – going for a short walk, filling out the university application, learning to be selfless in a relationship. Each action takes us to a new plateau from which the next challenge becomes visible. The process then continues.

Endurance athletes, those with the title "Doctor", husbands and wives in long-term successful relationships, and many others know that what once seemed completely unattainable is actually quite possible. Think of that the next time you look up into the sky.

Hope is the feeling you have that the feeling you have isn't permanent.

- Jean Kerr

Life can be tough. There are short term aggravations – the traffic jam, the dropped cell phone call, the slow cashier – and there are serious long term issues related to health, relationships, finances, etc. What can bring us hope during these times?

It is comforting to realize that the human spirit is amazingly resilient. Although the pain of some severe situations never completely leaves us, over time the negative feelings do diminish significantly. And those minor annoyances of everyday life are usually forgotten altogether.

Take heart. The challenges of today will seem less difficult as we journey into the future. And that's a reason to have hope.

Shepherds And Hired Hands

The greatest teacher who ever lived made an observation about the sheep industry. He said that there were two types of people in that business – the shepherds and the hired hands. The way to tell the difference between the two is to watch what happens when the wolf comes. The shepherds will stay and fight the wolf to protect the sheep. The hired hands will run for their lives.

We're not in the sheep business. So instead of calling them shepherds, let's call them "leaders."

And since we don't have wolves running around, the way to tell who is a leader is to watch what happens in particular situations ...

- Who honors a request to come in early or stay late under special circumstances?
- Who helps co-workers without being asked?
- Who cleans up after themselves or cleans up after someone else?
- Who makes sure that they are adhering to company policies, and helps others do so as well?

The list goes on and on.

Every organization needs leaders. But not everyone is a leader, nor would we want them to be. To keep day-to-day operations running smoothly, organizations also need doers who fit the culture, take ownership of the company's values and goals, and make significant contributions in supporting roles.

Shepherds and hired hands. Leaders and doers. Both are important to a business.

Tension, Teamwork, Leadership

Inter-departmental integration – that's a complicated-sounding phrase that means it's a business leader's job to keep the gears meshing and not grinding.

In any company there is tension between departments. If the tension is healthy, that's good. If the tension is not healthy, that's very bad. For example: Sales wants to tell the client "We'll finish it tomorrow," but Production says they need a week. Production asks for more and better equipment and people, but Finance and Resources replies "We can't afford that."

Most of these tensions work themselves out or are handled between the parties involved. If and when they don't, it's a leader's responsibility to find common ground. The leader may tell Sales that completing the project tomorrow is unreasonable but Production will have to make it happen in three days. In the case of equipment and people, leadership would take input from all sides, then set parameters within which the departments would get it done.

In each situation, leadership has the advantage of seeing the big picture and most likely knows information that the individual department representatives don't. And that's OK. The departments SHOULD mainly be concerned about their own interests and what makes them perform better. Sales should ALWAYS want to do things quicker in order to impress the customer. Production should ALWAYS want more time, equipment, and people in order to do a better job. Finance and Resources should ALWAYS want to preserve cash. That's the reason for the healthy tension.

As long as everyone has the same ultimate goal – profitability of the company – teamwork usually prevails. But if not, leadership kicks in and creates that complicated-sounding phrase ... inter-departmental integration.

A Closer Look At Leadership

Every person is a leader in some way. Each of us has been given a life to lead, and many people have additional responsibilities in their families, social circles, or careers. The following thoughts provide some basic principles about leadership.

Leaders First Lead Themselves
- They are engaged in some life management and time management process.
- They know how to prioritize, say "no", and live with margin.
- The only way to lead by example is to model the proper behavior.

Leaders Ask Questions
- Should the leader have all the answers, or ask all the questions?
  - Both, to a degree, but asking questions is the more important part.

Leaders Think
- They intentionally set aside time for no other purpose but to think.
- They try to find all the angles, holes, gaps, opportunities, etc. in a situation.

Leaders Prepare
- They avoid chaos and last minute scrambling like the plague.

Leaders Practice MBWA (Management By Walking Around)
- They know what's going on with the people and organizations they lead.

Leaders Observe
- As they MBWA they notice areas that need improvement as well as best practices.

Leaders Follow Up
- They don't assume that something got accomplished properly – or at all.

Leaders Take Responsibility, But Let Others Take Credit
- I messed up ... We could have done better ... You (He / She) aced it.

Leaders Look For Positive Qualities In Others
- They help the people around them grow and develop.

Leaders Share And Communicate
- They don't keep ideas or best practices to themselves.
- They distribute as much appropriate information as they possibly can.

Effective leaders are both rare and powerful. Use these guidelines to enhance your leadership abilities. Your value in life and business will increase dramatically.

Failure is only the opportunity to more intelligently begin again.

- Henry Ford

To be successful at everything the first time we do it is a human impossibility. This lack of initial success has two names. Some call it failure. Others call it education.

Armed with the education obtained by so-called failures, we are better equipped to make a new attempt at our goal. This time, we clearly see that one or more methods tried previously will not obtain the desired results. We determine not to repeat the actions that brought us that education. The cycle continues, and eventually we achieve our objective.

There is no short cut to success. Failure, better viewed as education, is a milestone along the way.

Your Highest And Best Use

A story goes that someone commenting on his beautiful *David* sculpture once asked Michelangelo, "It's as though he were an angel. How did you do that?" Michelangelo replied, "I saw the angel in the marble and I carved until I set him free."

Every person alive is like that marble. Within each man and woman are character traits waiting to be set free. How are those traits uncovered?

In the commercial real estate industry there is a concept called "highest and best use." Real estate professionals use this for the purpose of determining the value of a property.

Let's suppose there's a piece of land with a gas station on it. The commercial real estate appraisers do not necessarily consider the gas station when determining the value of the land. Instead, they look at that property imagining its highest and best use. Maybe a gas station truly is the best use of that location. But the best use could be an office building, a skyscraper, or an amusement park. The property appraisal is based on the lot's highest and best use, whatever that might be.

What is the highest and best use of a human being? Our list would probably include elements such as love, joy, peace, patience, kindness, goodness, faithfulness, gentleness, self-control, etc. How do these highest and best use traits develop? How is that angel within us released? Fortunately, there is a definite method that makes those things happen. It's happening all the time and it's a specific event that occurs. It's called life.

Life itself is causing growth. Every situation in a man or woman's life creates personal growth. Every circumstance he or she faces is carving the marble that is that person, releasing the angel of highest and best use.

For example, most of us would like to have more patience, but how does that happen? What carves patience into our lives? Consider the morning traffic jam. We can curse it, or we can understand what it really is. It's the carving of the marble to create patience in us, developing one or more of the necessary character traits to get us to our highest and best use.

This way of thinking can be expanded to every situation that occurs in life. We will then truly understand the Latin phrase *omnia causa fiunt*: "Everything happens for a reason." The reason, as you now know, is to develop the highest and best use of our lives.

Growing. Pains.

Most people have heard the phrase "growing pains." It's an interesting concept. Just about everyone wants to grow – professionally, health-related, in relationships, and in other ways. But pain … that's not so attractive.

If we are going to grow in any area of life, however, we will experience pain. It's a simple fact.

There are many types of pain. Physical pain can be part of growth – just ask a teething baby or anyone who works out at a gym or trains for a marathon. There's also the emotional pain we feel when we're just not understanding something, or the psychological pain of moving out of our comfort zones.

I can't put money in the bank, lose a pound, or improve a friendship without denying myself of my own desires once in awhile. Ouch! In order to master a new skill or overcome a challenging obstacle, I'm going to have to invest time, study, practice, fall down, and maybe even embarrass myself. Ouch again!

The good news is that on the other side of the pain is growth. Eventually, I'll gain that ability, become more adept in that situation, have more knowledge of that topic, etc.

Think of any goal. It will not be accomplished without some form of pain. The degree to which a person is willing to endure discomfort will largely determine whether or not the goal is achieved.

The Way You Pour A Cup Of Tea

It's amazing how much we can learn from simple things all around us. Of course I'm talking about tea.

Consider this saying: "The way you pour a cup of tea is the way you do everything."

Isn't that profound?

A person who is responsible in some areas of life will be equally responsible in other areas. If someone cheats on the golf scorecard, however, there's a good chance that he or she shouldn't be given the club money box.

This proverb is so deep in its minimalism that not much needs to be said to elaborate on it. To be a person of integrity means to bring an uncompromising approach to every task in our courts, from big to small. Even pouring a cup of tea.

The Hard Work Of Simplicity

Many years ago, a friend invited me to join him in seeing blues guitar legend B. B. King in concert. We jumped in his classic Cutlass convertible and took off, making sure to get there early because of the open seating policy, which turned out to be open standing. The venue was small, and we found a spot right up front.

B. B. was great, of course. And being so close, plus being a long-time guitar player myself, I recognized all of his chord progressions. By the end of the night I had them memorized and was convinced that I could play the blues, pretty much just like King.

When I got home, I grabbed my guitar, started with a barred G 7th, and went on from there. But to my surprise, it didn't sound anything like what I'd heard earlier. I was shocked. It looked so easy when I was watching B. B. King. What was wrong?

The answer can be found in the tens of thousands of hours that B. B. has spent perfecting what he does. Tiny improvements, but hundreds of them, until arriving at a sound so incredible that he's famous all over the world. That's the hard work that makes it look simple.

The greatest proof that anything you or I produce is excellent, and as good as it can be, is that we've made it seem easy. That can only be accomplished by thinking, revising, taking a stern look, digging deeper, making more improvements, tearing a project apart and restarting from scratch, exposing our drafts to scrutiny, humbly accepting constructive criticism, and more.

When we've endured all the agony and arrived at a final product, somebody who barely knows anything about our area of expertise will look at what we've done and think "I could do that. It looks so easy." And he'll really believe it – until he goes home and picks up his guitar.

To Get Smart, Play Dumb

If you want to learn new things, here's some advice: Play Dumb.

For example, let's say that my computer is not printing properly and I call a technician. If I say "I think my printer driver is corrupt. Can you help me reinstall it?" I sound like I know what the problem is. The advice I get, therefore, will likely be limited to that one area. But if I play dumb and say, "My computer's not printing properly. Do you have any idea what could be wrong?," the technician may go through a few possible causes other than the printer driver, and I'll learn in the process.

Of course there are times when one knows a lot about an issue and wants to ask very specific questions. But the "Play Dumb Method Of Gaining Information" is a good one that lifelong learners employ to become even better. Don't be afraid to use it.

How To Become An Expert

There's no mystery to what makes someone an expert. It's actually quite simple. Typically, that person has remained devoted to a particular field for a significant amount of time. He or she has learned about something specific, done it personally, and continued long enough to see and handle many common and uncommon nuances.

To become an expert then, you just have to be who you are. The key is to stay consistent and never stop progressing. Sadly, most people's forward motion ends when they finish school, settle into a job, or find status quo in some other way. Continual improvement, on the other hand, leads to expert status.

It's been said that if you read for 30 minutes a day, you'll reach the top 5% of your industry within two years. It might require even less reading than that.

Another basic principle of self development is to find someone who exemplifies the personal attributes, knowledge, etc. you would like to have and ask that person to train you. Such people are all around us. As the saying goes, "When the student is ready, the teacher appears."

Then there's the famous story of the tourist in New York who asked a passerby "How do I get to Carnegie Hall?" The person replied, "Practice, practice, practice." If you want to develop your professional skills, start taking some steps and keep at it.

Those who never stop learning, doing, and experiencing move quickly to levels of authority. They gain recognition, noteworthy reputations, and a prestigious title: Expert.

Full Speed Ahead

On August 5, 1864, Civil War Union Admiral David Glasgow Farragut ordered his fleet of battle ships to charge Mobile Bay. The bay was filled with floating enemy mines, which in those days were called "torpedoes."

From his flagship, USS *Hartford*, Admiral Farragut gave the command "Full speed ahead." When the lead ship, USS *Tecumseh*, struck a torpedo and began to sink, the second ship in the column started to pull back. Farragut then climbed the rigging of the *Hartford* and screamed out, "What's the trouble?" to which he received the reply, "Sir, the torpedoes." It was then that Farragut uttered his famous saying, "Damn the torpedoes. Full speed ahead."

There are always torpedoes in the waters of life and business. Many individuals and companies retreat as they see others sinking. Some, however, choose a different approach. While not being ignorant of the danger, they nevertheless declare "Full speed ahead" despite the torpedoes.

Thank you, Admiral Farragut, for a lesson in facing challenges.

Fear Of Success

Fear. It comes in many varieties, from the universal fear of bodily harm to rare but very real diseases such as arithmophobia, the fear of numbers. Sadly, one strange and not uncommon condition is the fear of success.

Success can be scary for many reasons. For one, it brings with it a journey into the unknown. A person who has never before had to navigate a close relationship, function as a newly-promoted supervisor, or manage excess dollars will have to learn additional skills. The safe route would be to remain status quo and not deal with any of that.

Friends, family, and co-workers might become resentful of the successful person. Misunderstandings sometimes occur which can be awkward to resolve. Second guessing, judgments, and even accusations may follow. All of this is avoidable by just leaving things as they are.

Success raises the bar, possibly making the future more challenging. The person who endures a grueling 20-week marathon training plan and accomplishes his goal to complete the race in four hours will likely have to embark on an even more aggressive regimen for the next one as the goal gets tougher. Keeping expectations low would be much easier.

So why bother overcoming the fear of success? Because the rewards are so worth it. Personal and professional growth are fulfilling on many levels, and scaling new heights in any area of life is euphoric.

Fearing success is understandable. Tackle that feeling head on and enjoy the outcome.

Ouch and Yay!

Two individual words speak volumes about adapting to changing times and challenges.

The first one is the word "Pain." Ouch! All of us are likely to feel some pain at times. It may be the pain of getting paid for fewer hours if things are slow at the office. Or the pain of staying late or coming in on a Saturday to impress a client. It may be the pain of price concessions to stay competitive, putting off buying or doing something we really want, admitting we were wrong, facing a new challenge, or many other situations.

The other word is "Opportunity." Yay! There's always great opportunity for businesses willing to dig deeper, work harder, and add value. There's the opportunity to be strategic partners to customers and provide the innovative solutions they need.

In our personal lives, there's the opportunity to show family, friends, and acquaintances that they are cared about as people, as some of them might just want a listening ear. There's the opportunity to overcome obstacles, and take our lives in new directions.

And there's the opportunity to cultivate truly first class relationships all across the board.

Yes, the times are always changing and the challenges keep coming. Those who accept some pain as part of the price of progress will uncover a great deal of opportunity.

Three Questions To Ask Yourself

When faced with a situation that's bigger than you can easily handle, break it down into smaller pieces.

Sit somewhere comfortable with just a pen and a pad of paper. Using a computer can be OK, as long as you don't let it become distracting. Ask yourself three questions, and answer them with whatever jumps to mind. The questions are:

- What are the issues?
- What am I doing well?
- What can I do differently?

That's it. It's amazing how deeply into your thinking and your life you can get with just a pen, paper, those three questions, and even just a few minutes to spare.

Risk Or Foolishness?

In order for people to experience personal development, they have to take risks. But when is an activity a risk, and when is it foolishness? A few criteria can help answer this question.

Preparation. Running a marathon involves an element of risk. There is much that could go wrong, from the simple embarrassment of not being able to finish, to serious physical problems. Most people who tackle this feat do so only after several months of specific training. When they get to the starting line, they're ready. The 26.2 miles will still be challenging and full of unknowns, but the preparation will have made it a reasonable undertaking.

Upside. Some situations are full of potential. Unleashing it often requires going outside the comfort zone. Pain, failure, humiliation, loss – all are real possibilities. But if the payoff could be big enough, it may make sense to take the leap and see what happens.

Downside. Before taking a risk, it's appropriate to ask "What might happen if this doesn't pan out?" If lack of complete success carries severe implications to the individual, to others, or to the organization, then perhaps the risk isn't worth it. Sometimes it's better to play it a little safer. On the other hand, there can be very real negative consequences to not taking a risk. Missed opportunities and lives wasted in the status quo become bitter pills.

Calculation. No general goes to battle without first considering whether he, with his army, can defeat the other general's leadership and army. Before stepping into new territory, it's essential to weigh all the factors. Victory is never guaranteed, but certain loss can most always be avoided.

Risks are necessary ingredients of a life that performs to full capacity. Be prepared, consider both the upside and downside, and spend some time in careful calculation. That's the way to keep risks from becoming too dangerous, and instead realize their power as tools for producing positive results.

Achieving Excellence

Excellence requires discipline in a few very distinct areas.

First is the exercise of thinking. Before starting a new task or project, literally stop and think. Ask yourself questions, such as "What's the objective of this project?", "What are the obstacles?", "What are the absolute non-negotiables that must be included or excluded?"

Just the act of thinking will likely bring up more questions. You may then need to do some research or ask someone for more information. And by thinking you arrive at answers. Those answers provide a framework for what you're about to do.

Conclusions formed during the thinking process must be incorporated into your efforts. There can be no compromises. It's tempting to say "Oh well, it's not really that important." But if your thinking has revealed a need, it IS that important.

After some deep thinking and appropriate efforts, you'll have a finished product, right? Wrong! You'll have a first draft. The next step is to revise it. This means looking at the output with a very critical eye. "Does this accomplish all the objectives? Is it the best it can be? Is there any way I can make it better?" are just a few of the tests to conduct – not just on the first draft, but on the many drafts that come along during the revision process. Seeking the advice of a friend or coworker can be helpful as well. Each time you revise, the output gets a little better.

Finally, when you feel that what you've done can't be improved any more, it's ready to be turned over to the next person in line. If that person suggests additional improvements, so much the better. After all, everyone has the same goal: excellence. And that only comes from a lot of discipline.

Back To Basics

The Green Bay Packers of the late 1960s may have been the best football team ever. Their coach, Vince Lombardi, is legendary. A story is told that the team entered the club house for their first practice after winning the Super Bowl the season before. The room got quiet as the world's best football players sat in front of the world's greatest coach. How did Vince Lombardi start the team's training for the new year? He held up a football and said, "Gentlemen, this is a football."

No matter how good you are, you must always get back to basics. Especially after a distraction – large or small – getting back to basics is without question the most important thing to do.

Many successful businesses abide by basics such as: Asking the "Why Are We Doing This?" question ... Serving the internal and external customer ... Exceeding expectations ... Looking for the next step ... etc. Each of us also has basics in our own particular occupations.

And then there are personal basics. These might include time management or effectiveness tools, organization techniques, prioritizing, staying focused, devoting attention to important relationships and the like.

Identify the basics in your professional and personal life. Then, when you get distracted for any reason, go back to them. It's your way of saying to yourself, "Gentlemen (and ladies), this is a football."

Have A Heart

The story of The Wizard Of Oz that is shown on television is an adaptation of a book entitled *The Wonderful Wizard Of Oz*, written by L. Frank Baum in 1900. The initial volume was so popular that Baum wound up writing 14 books about Oz until his health got too bad in 1920. Book number 12 is *The Tin Woodman Of Oz*. It tells about the character we call The Tinman.

Nick Chopper was a wood chopper. He and a Munchkin girl named Nimmie Amee fell in love and wanted to get married. But there was a problem – Nimmie was the personal servant of The Wicked Witch Of The East. The Witch didn't want to lose her servant, and she didn't much care for love, so she put a spell on Nick Chopper's axe.

The spell caused the ax to cut off Nick Chopper's arm. But in Oz nobody dies, so this didn't kill Nick. He went to the tinsmith and had a new arm made from tin. The ax then cut off all of Nick's other limbs and even his head, but the tinsmith always made new tin limbs for him and a tin neck to hold his head back on. Finally, the ax cut Nick's torso. The tinsmith made a torso out of tin, but did not include within it a heart.

All was well for awhile. The Tin Woodman, as he was now called, was very productive, because his tin limbs never got tired. The Munchkin maiden was thrilled with all the great things about a tin man (she lists a bunch of them in the book, such as he could dance for hours and not get tired). She still wanted to marry him and even said, "I shall take pride in being the wife of the only tin woodman in the world."

Did The Tin Woodman marry Nimmie? In his own words, he states, "No, I did not. She said she still loved me, but I found that I no longer loved her. My tin body contained no heart, and without a heart no one can love."

This is a great lesson on the human condition. Without a heart, we can accomplish much. We might be more productive and find new ways to give ourselves what we think we want. But without a heart we miss out on the greater experiences of life. We would not feel emotional pain – true – but we wouldn't feel joy either. And the biggest consequence is that we wouldn't be able to love.

My advice is simple: Always have a heart. Always listen to and follow your heart when it leads you on the path of love. I'm sure that even the Wizard Of Oz would agree.

The Marathon Of Life

I was fortunate to run the Bank of America Chicago Marathon in 2013. I was pleased, disappointed, and brought to a place of reflection. Pleased that I beat my previous best marathon time by four and a half minutes and my previous Chicago by eleven minutes. Disappointed because I thought I was going to do a little better. And brought to reflection for several reasons.

A marathon, like any major accomplishment, is not a single event. I was on a specific training plan for 20 weeks prior. Every workout was part of the whole. And just about all of them, though sometimes grueling, were enjoyable in some way. Certainly there were days when I didn't want to get up at 4:30 A.M. to run or crosstrain, but the sense of achievement when the day's goal was met was worth every minute.

I also interacted with some great friends along the way. We were all preparing for the Chicago race together back home in Ft. Lauderdale. We swapped e-mails, text messages, phone calls. We shouted encouragements on the roads and at the track. Our relationships deepened, because few dynamics bring people closer than mutual suffering. And we rejoiced together at the finish line.

Then there was the Chicago experience itself. Several days enjoying the city. The excitement of being with 45,000 runners. The cheers of an estimated two million spectators. And meeting a milestone that I thought would be impossible just a few years before was deeply rewarding.

The 2013 Chicago Marathon was tremendous. But it's only a metaphor for so many facets of life. Each day there are triumphs and disappointments. Yet if we look at the bigger picture – if we reflect on everything that brought us to that day, the people we've touched and who have helped us, and the overall events themselves, we find that profound things are taking place. We've all tapped more of our own potential. And that's a race everybody wins.

You can't help getting older, but you don't have to get old.
                                                    - George Burns

Two men, aged 96 and 91, were heatedly discussing politics. It eventually became clear that neither would persuade the other to his point of view. Suddenly, the older man turned to the younger and said in frustration, "I used to have the same shallow, immature opinion you do – back when I was your age."

There is no good alternative to adding numbers to our years on Earth. But alternatives to getting old abound. There are new challenges to be tackled, lessons to be learned, personal areas to improve, and goals to achieve. And perhaps one of the greatest benefits is the vast experience that we can pass along to others.

People who make the most of life refuse to become old, even as they inevitably grow older.

Thomas Watson, Mr. Think

Business leaders know the importance of getting people to think. Peter Drucker, the guru of management, said this was one of the two major traits he looked for before promoting someone to an executive position. And probably the most famous proponent of the "Think" concept was Thomas Watson.

Thomas Watson started his career as a teacher around the year 1891. He lasted one day, then went to accounting school and took a position as a bookkeeper in a butcher shop for $6 a week. He was so impressed with the store's cash register that he became a salesperson for the company – National Cash Register, or NCR. Watson was great in sales, earning $100 per week at the age of 25 in 1899.

Watson left NCR and joined the Computing Tabulating Recording Corporation as General Manager in May 1914. At that time, the company produced $9 million in annual revenues and had 1,300 employees. Ten years later, he renamed the company International Business Machines … IBM. Under Watson's leadership, IBM became so dominant that the federal government filed an antitrust suit against them in 1952. When Watson died in 1956, holding the position of CEO, IBM's revenues were $897 million and the company had 72,500 employees.

Thomas Watson is known for the slogan he brought to IBM. It was one word: THINK. A magazine article in 1940 said "This word is on the most conspicuous wall of every room in every IBM building. Each employee carries a THINK notebook in which to record inspirations. The company stationery, matches, scratch pads all bear the inscription, THINK. A monthly magazine called 'Think' is distributed to the employees."

If you were to buy an IBM laptop computer years later (eventually sold under the name Lenovo), do you know what it would be called? That's right, a "ThinkPad." And that's something to think about.

Think About This

We all have the ability to think. Sometimes, however, we just don't do it, even though it could really help us grow. Why not? A few possibilities come to mind.

We don't take the time to think. Thinking is an intentional event. If you or I are given a project to accomplish, we can either jump in and get at it, or we can think first. The truth is that thinking IS getting at it – and probably in the most effective way. Certainly we shouldn't spend ALL our time thinking. That's called paralysis by analysis. A little time spent thinking, however, can pay off big down the road.

We don't see the value that thinking brings. The reason we don't take time is that we may not really believe there's value in thinking. Then the mistake occurs, or the obvious is overlooked and we say to ourselves "If I had stopped for five minutes and thought about this project, I'm sure that pitfall would have occurred to me." Much better to realize the value of thought before the negative impact hits.

We're multi-taskers. Probably few people remember Windows 3.0. Its release in 1990 introduced the phrase "multi-task." It meant that a computer could now run more than one application at the same time. Wow! I no longer had to close WordPerfect before opening QuattroPro.

Then multi-tasking stopped being only digital and became organic. In other words, human beings started seeing how many things they could do at once. This has become the enemy of effective thinking. When multi-tasking takes the place of focus, we're in trouble. Study after study shows that people must focus in order to be truly productive. Or, as the proverb says, "He who chases two rabbits catches none."

Take time to think, see the value in thinking, and remember to focus rather than trying to cover too many bases at once. You'll be better for it. I really think so.

Thinking ... Let Me Count The Ways

There are several different ways to think. Conscious, subconscious, left brain and right brain.

Experts tell us that we can think with our conscious minds and with our subconscious minds. Conscious, intentional thinking is the first step. Experience confirms that once we do that, something amazing happens. As we step away, new thoughts come to us when we least expect it, sometimes hours or days later. The more we plan ahead and discipline ourselves to be ready, the more those subconscious thoughts occur and reach the surface where we can benefit from them.

There is also left brain / right brain thinking. The left side of the brain thinks in words, logic, analysis, and fact, while the right side of the brain ponders images, feelings, and emotion. Both are important. If we practice these two types of thought, we can learn to call on one or the other in different circumstances. We can even go back and forth, and get them to work together. It's a very helpful skill.

Learn to engage all the resources of your mind in a controlled manner. There you'll find a powerful resource for growing personally and professionally.

Harnessing Thoughts

Scientists tell us that thoughts are the result of neurons sending and reacting to electromechanical signaling. I'm not sure what that means, but I do know that getting thoughts to come to our minds is more than a vague, ethereal mystery that just happens. We can be intentional about the activity of thinking.

First, identify a situation that should have some thinking applied to it. It's easy to miss this, since we all move so quickly. Developing this habit, however, is extremely helpful.

Once you've decided to think about something, create the environment in which you can think. If it's impossible to think in the living room, because the TV remote control is too tempting or the kids won't leave you alone, then go to another part of the house, a park, or a coffee shop. If you find it difficult to think at your desk, a conference room or library might be a good environment. Do you like music or silence? Scented candles? As Plato said, "Know thyself," then set up the environment that will help you think.

Next, deal with any obvious distractions. This might mean making that phone call that's nagging you, clearing a few e-mails, reviewing a memo for which someone else is waiting, or telling others that you'll be out of touch for a certain length of time.

Have a pen and paper ready. Thoughts enter and leave the mind quickly. You want to be able to capture them.

Then be still and allow yourself to think about that specific situation.

Before you totally complete the project, get away from it for a few minutes. Maybe walk down the hall, eat a healthy snack, or get a drink of water. Then take one last look at whatever was the object of your thought.

You'll be amazed at the results of this exercise. Intentional thinking is very powerful.

We can only do what we think we can do. We can be only what we think we can be. We can have only what we think we can have. What we do, what we are, what we have, all depend upon what we think.

- Robert Collier

Look around you. Every object you see began with a thought. Likewise, every personal accomplishment, every work of art, every act of self improvement – each one started with just a thought. With thoughts, we literally create something out of nothing.

But thoughts can also be limiting. When we think we can not achieve certain goals, we set barriers for ourselves that are quite difficult to overcome.

Harness your thoughts. When you catch yourself thinking negatively, replace that mindset with visions of victory in whatever circumstance you find yourself. The power of thought is enormous. Use it to your advantage.

Take Your Time

Look at a clock. Seriously, right now, stop what you're doing and stare at a clock for one minute. Then come back and keep reading.

Guess what ... you just spent a minute of your life looking at a clock. A precious minute of your life is gone. Was that a cruel trick? Maybe not, because if you grasp this important truth, your life can be positively and profoundly affected forever.

Here it is: The way you spend your time is the way you spend your life. Please repeat that last sentence until it sinks in.

Time is a finite resource. People say "There aren't enough hours in the day." Whether there are or not makes no difference. The fact is that there are exactly 24 of them, each containing 60 minutes. Like any finite resource, the more efficiently we can utilize it, the better.

Time is the true equalizer. Everyone gets exactly the same amount each hour. Some individuals are born with greater talent or money, but no one on Earth, regardless of how rich or gifted, has more or less time in a given week.

Shakespeare said, "nothing 'gainst Time's scythe can make defense." That could almost be considered depressing and morbid. Much better to accept the quote's truth and dismiss any intention of fighting time. Instead, make time an ally, embrace it, and become a master at its use.

There is incredible importance and power in this thing called time.

Five Seconds = One Hour

Most people wish they had more time. At least that's what they say. But often they waste huge amounts of time on activities that do not move them toward their life's vision and goals. Certainly, we all need rest, recreation, and fun. Our goals should in fact reflect that. But much time is simply squandered with little value.

Since creating more time is impossible, the best we can do is use the time that we do have more productively. And there's a really easy way to discover an entire hour in every ten-hour period.

If a person saves 30 seconds every five minutes, that adds up to one hour every ten hours. Stated another way, if we can eliminate 30 seconds of wasted time every five minutes, we'll accomplish in nine hours what used to take us ten.

Start opening your eyes and mind to the things you might do that waste a few seconds here and there.

This essay could be made a bit longer, but I'm going to end it here. That means you're several seconds ahead right now!

Three Little Words For Time Management

Some of the best time management tactics come in bite-size portions – all the better to save valuable time. This series of three-word phrases cuts to the chase with tips you can quickly apply.

- A Scary Thought – The way we spend our time is the way we spend our lives. Keep that truth top of mind and you'll be more careful as to your use of time.

- First Things First – Otherwise you'll never get to them.

- Make A Plan – Don't live life haphazardly or reactively. Know what you want to accomplish for the day or the hour.

- Use A List – Master Lists and To Do Lists keep people organized. Checklists provide focus, especially in stressful situations.

- Write It Down – How much time has been wasted because of something forgotten? A piece of paper can't forget.

- Hard Things First – Get that tough task or project out of the way and you'll feel much better and more able to tackle other challenges.

- Easy Things First – Sometimes you can get several easy items off your desk in just a few minutes. This gives you a lot more space, on your desk and in your brain, for other tasks and projects.

- Stop And Think – Before heading out on an errand, ask yourself "Am I forgetting anything?" or "Is there something else I could do in that part of town?"

There you have a few time management thoughts. I'd share some more, but for now, the three little words on my mind are "Back To Work."

Productivity ... Yes And No

People often feel that the word "Yes" is the most important factor of meeting goals and achieving personal growth. For example, we think that we have to say "Yes, I'll exercise. Yes, I'll save money. Yes, I'll read that book. Yes, I'll call that person." Etc. But here's a secret that great implementers share ... The word "No" is actually more important than "Yes."

Those who are overcommitted and overwhelmed often cite "I just can't say 'No'" as the root of their problems. But the truth is that these same men and women are saying "No" all the time. They just spell it Y-E-S.

Every Yes is actually many more Nos. So whenever a person says "Yes", which is so easy to do, he or she is actually saying "No" dozens of times.

"Yes, I'll go to the movie" is "No, I won't invest those two hours reading, exercising, talking to my spouse, learning something new, etc." "Yes, I'll buy that" is "No, I won't buy this other thing, or save the money, or use these resources to help someone in need." And on and on it goes.

Knowing when to say "No" is a very advanced personal growth skill. But before you think about that, there are dozens of videos on the Internet of dogs sneezing. Maybe you should watch those instead ... what do you say?

The Positive Results Of "No"

When faced with demands on our time or other resources, there are two possible responses, "Yes" or "No." Let's look at some aspects of saying "No."

A certain man had two sons. He asked them both to do an errand. The first son said, "Sure Pop, I'll do that," but he got distracted and the errand went by the wayside. The second son replied, "Sorry, I don't think I'll get to it today, Dad." Later he was able to eliminate some unessentials from his schedule and accomplish the errand after all. Which son did what his father wanted?

This story points out one of the values of the word "No." It can get us off the hook. Then if we don't perform the task in question, no problem – we haven't disappointed anyone, cast doubt upon our credibility, or harmed our reputation. Of course at times No is not acceptable, such as when the boss or customer asks for help or someone has a true need. But in many cases declining a request is necessary as it may be virtually impossible to do otherwise. There is absolutely nothing wrong that.

Saying "No" does not make us less productive or responsive. It can actually make us more so. That's because every No to one thing is a Yes to something else. A reply of No to an interruption or distraction can be a Yes to a higher priority or commitment.

No to the TV sitcom can mean Yes to helping a friend balance his checkbook. No to mindless video games can be Yes to time with the family. No to being a couch potato or eating that donut may be Yes to taking a walk or snacking on a banana. The same holds true in the workplace where No to someone's request that you stop everything and read an article can mean Yes to finishing the proposal, the marketing plan, or the report that is dangerously close to deadline. Like the second son in the story above, perhaps the situation will change and you'll read the article later anyway.

Those who wish to live to their full potential must master the art of saying "No". Positive results will follow.

The Yes And No Monkey

How can you tell when to say "Yes" and when to say "No"? There aren't any absolute rules, but an article by William Oncken, Jr. and Donald L. Wass can provide some guidelines.

In its November-December 1999 issue, *Harvard Business Review* published a paper entitled "Who's Got The Monkey?" It became the basis of a bestselling business book, *The One Minute Manager Meets the Monkey*. Oncken and Wass said that there are three kinds of time: Boss-imposed; System-imposed; and Self-imposed.

Boss-imposed time, the authors explained, is used to accomplish activities that the boss requires. Neglecting these can result in unfavorable consequences. System-imposed time is used to provide the support needed to keep the system operating. Saying "No" to these can also bring adverse results. Since negative responses to the first two types of time can be dire, it is the third type, Self-imposed time where we must focus in the pursuit of Yes and No.

Self-imposed time is time that we use to do those things that we either originate on our own or are asked by others to do, but that are not requirements from our boss or the system. Still, the way we use this time is extremely important, since poor choices here will result in less productivity and effectiveness, leading to unwanted consequences long term.

To illustrate which activities deserve "Yes" and which deserve "No", Oncken and Wass used the analogy of a monkey. Any time there is a transaction between two people, they said, there is an invisible monkey present. The person who leaves the exchange with the next step in his or her court is said to have the monkey. (Hence the title of the article: "Who's Got The Monkey?")

The objective is to only take those monkeys that truly belong on our own backs or that we intentionally want there. Boss-imposed and System-imposed monkeys must be accepted. But Self-imposed monkeys should be considered carefully.

It's all a matter of yes and no.

iwuzjusgonna

There's a common practice in society and at many businesses as well. It's called "iwuzjusgonna."

Iwuzjusgonna takes place when a person is asked about the status of a task that is pending, and he or she answers "I was just going to do that."

When people say, "iwuzjusgonna", in most cases they truly ARE planning to accomplish that project or task *just then* ... along with a few dozen other things that they had thoughts of accomplishing *just then*. But since nobody can complete more than one item at a time, something had to get pushed to the back burner. The task that was the subject in question was one of many "iwuzjusgonnas" that were somewhere on the plate.

The root causes of this malady are disorganization and a bit of procrastination. People who are intentional about working within a system and doing things now rather than putting them off have far fewer instances of saying "I was just going to do that." It's probably not possible to eliminate those words altogether, but with a few habit changes, they can be minimized substantially.

That's all the time I have on this topic. The To Do List beckons, filled with stuff I need to handle ... before someone asks about it.

Make Your Yes Yes

The greatest book ever written contains this advice: "Make your yes yes and your no no." That sounds pretty simple, but it's very often violated.

The degree to which we show integrity in our "Yes" and our "No" can be plotted on a continuum:

- The best scenario is to promise something a little better than people expect, then exceed their expectations. Example: If some friends ask you to help them move on a Saturday morning, and you already have plans for the afternoon, you might say "Yes, but I won't be able to stay the whole time." If they reply "Just two hours would be great," agree to help for two and a half hours, and then actually stay for three. This principle applies to deadlines, fees, any type of favor, commitments, etc. Of course doing this is not always possible, but when you can, it's powerful.

- In the middle of the continuum are times when we simply perform as we said we would. No fanfare. No drama. This is the baseline of integrity.

- Sadly, sometimes we say we're going to do something and then we don't follow through. All of us have been there. It's a symptom of being human. The best course of action when we drop the ball is to simply apologize – with no conditions or explanations attached – and promptly fulfill what we said we'd do if at all possible, or make restitution if appropriate.

Being intentional about your yes and your no, and then living up to those words, will make all your interactions – professionally and personally – run more smoothly. And we can all say "Yes" to that.

Mastering Yes Or No – A Review

The benefits of being intentional about your use of the words "Yes" and "No" are substantial. The quick review below provides a snapshot of guidelines for getting it right:

- "Make your yes yes and your no no" is wise advice from the greatest book ever written. To do so shows integrity and builds trust. To fail in this simple exercise erodes reputations. So when you say you're going to tackle something large or small, make good on those words.

- Even better than fulfilling commitments is exceeding other people's expectations in the process. This means that you accomplish the objective quicker, better, or less expensively (if what you're doing involves a fee) than expected.

- If something falls through the cracks, you must not justify or make excuses, no matter how reasonable or even noble was the cause of your shortfall. The best course of action is a simple apology with no caveats such as "if" or "but", followed by completing the task whenever that's still possible.

- Sometimes "No" is a better response to a request than "Yes." "No" is not an indication of failure or minimal capacity. Your perspective should be that every "No" to one thing is a "Yes" to something better … just as many times a "Yes" to one thing is a "No" to something that would have been better.

- How can you tell when to say "Yes" and when to say "No"? One way is by understanding the analogy of the monkey, as written in a *Harvard Business Review* article by William Oncken, Jr. and Donald L. Wass. Anytime there is a transaction between two people, the one who leaves with the next step in his or her court has the monkey. The goal is to gladly accept any monkey that is rightfully yours, while turning away monkeys that belong to other people; or that you can turn away without negative consequences; or that are not beneficial to your life.

- Three types of time – a.k.a. monkeys – compete for attention.

These are Boss-imposed, System-imposed, and Self-imposed. The first two must be taken seriously and carry negative consequences if violated. The last category is discretionary and offers opportunities for true "Yes" and "No" decision making that can result in greater or lesser efficiency and productivity.

There isn't an absolute answer to every "Yes" and "No" question that confronts us. But these guidelines should certainly help.

Black Holes

The phrase "black hole" entered pop culture after physicist John Wheeler coined the term in 1969. A black hole, we were told, was a spot in space-time from which nothing could escape. Scientists warned that large portions of matter, maybe even planet Earth, could be sucked into one of these and be gone forever.

There's not much you and I can do about what happens in the heavenlies, but a similar phenomenon exists in business which we can control. This type of black hole occurs when a person is assigned or voluntarily takes on a task and then goes silent on it. The task has entered a black hole.

Sometimes you have no choice as to what winds up on your plate. The boss or the system make demands on your time. Tasks in those categories are rightfully yours and require your attention.

Discretionary, self-imposed time is where you can avoid tasks that might end up as black holes. This means, for example, that when someone sends you an e-mail that doesn't absolutely require your action, you simply reply "Thanks. That's interesting," instead of adding "I'll find some more info on that topic and get back to you." The last phrase puts a commitment on your shoulders which you'll then need to handle lest it become a black hole.

Does that mean you shouldn't volunteer to go beyond duties that are clearly in your court? No! Extra efforts that exceed expectations are great. But when you raise your hand, you must follow through, or you'll have made matters worse.

And that leads to the second, and much more highly advisable, way to eliminate black holes: Just intentionally accomplish that to which you've committed, and in a reasonable amount of time.

Leave the black holes in outer space, and keep them away from your to-do list.

Two Powerful Tools

Two incredibly effective tools for making good use of your time are probably within a few feet of you right now. Using them, however, requires a great deal of discipline. The tools are the waste basket and the Delete key.

Every e-mail does not require a response. Every article does not have to be read, nor every survey completed. Likewise, computer files do not need to be kept indefinitely, where they'll simply clutter your digital storage system and your mind. These are all prime opportunities to use the Delete key.

Is there a stack of old mail on your desk? Trade journals from a year ago? Notes from the seminar you attended when you were first learning your job? Waste baskets come in very handy.

Imagine the time you'll save, and the increase in your productivity, when you press Delete one hundred or more times and toss a few pounds of paper in the waste basket. You'll see just how powerful those tools can be. Use them to make your life more effective.

Urgency Addiction

Urgency addiction. It shows its head when everything in an organization or a person's life becomes urgent. The result is constant chaos.

Yes, sometimes urgency is unavoidable. When the call comes from a customer who wants to change an order that's about to ship, urgency will kick in. So, always ask the question "Is this situation really urgent?" If so, do whatever it takes.

If the matter is not urgent, the following tips may help.

- Set appointments, instead of having impromptu meetings.

  Showing up unannounced at someone's desk for an unscheduled talk forces that person to stop what he or she is doing and shift gears. That can make the person feel disoriented. Much better to ask "Can we get together in 20 minutes to discuss a new project?" The person then has an opportunity to adjust his or her thinking, perhaps finish a consuming task, etc.

- Cover more than one topic at a time.
  When possible, put off sitting down with someone until you have a few topics to discuss. This will reduce the number of meetings, and make them more productive as well.

- Have someone's full attention before presenting information.
  Information that is shared while passing in the hallway can upset someone's equilibrium and is often misunderstood. If a coworker is headed to make a photocopy or find something in a file, that's probably what's on his or her mind. Being stopped on the way and asked a question or told something important is almost always a recipe for confusion. It's better to talk to that person while you're both able to focus and look each other in the eye.

These are just three techniques for overcoming urgency addiction in an organization. The next time potential chaos strikes, take a deep breath and review them again.

Time Management, Three More Little Words

Here are a few more three-word phrases that quickly spotlight key principles for using time efficiently.

- Do It Now – Procrastination is a mortal enemy of effectiveness. Some time management experts say that anything that can be done in two minutes or less should be done right now.

- Do It Later – Distractions can be just as deadly as procrastination. For example, you don't have to drop everything just because the mail arrived. If you're on a roll with a project, it's best to stick with it.

- Don't Do It – Ask yourself "What would happen if I never did this?" If the answer is "Nothing", don't do it.

- Ask For Help – Is there someone who could easily give you information or assistance that could lessen your time investment in this project? People are usually glad to help.

- Farm It Out – Maybe you can give the whole project to someone else. It may even be worth paying a fee if someone's involvement will save a lot of your time.

- Tie It Up – Finish the project completely. You'll be much more productive as you tackle your next task.

- Mix It Up – Winston Churchill said "A change is as good as a rest."

- Keep At It – As long as you're moving, you'll get there. When we stop making forward progress, we lose a lot of time.

- Have Some Fun – True effectiveness includes doing things that re-energize us and prepare us for the next period of hard work. Find what you love to do and allow yourself to do it.

There it is, time management tips in bite-size portions. After all, Less Is More.

Don't wait for extraordinary opportunities. Seize common opportunities and make them great.

- Orison S. Marsden

Some people feel that life has granted them few or no opportunities. Is that true? Opportunities come in all shapes and sizes. There are opportunities to profit in business, to show kindness to strangers, to develop personally, or to express love to family. Just opening your eyes in the morning presents a whole array of opportunities.

To ignore all but the most grandiose opportunities is a great mistake, and a great loss. In fact, our most notable gains generally come from many small steps in the right direction, taken over a period of time, rather than from one huge forward leap. Each step is the result of a positive response to what might have seemed like just a common opportunity.

When was the last time an opportunity crossed your path? It could be that you've already received many of them today.

Continuous Improvement

Kaizen. It's an ancient word that means "continuous improvement." Here's how it works.

Step 1 = Identify a standard. Typically this standard will align with some goal or will solve a problem.

Step 2 = Establish a system, policy, or procedure to achieve the standard.

Step 3 = Identify deviations from the standard. These will be situations that are not following the system, or that are not adequately covered by the system.

Step 4 = Address and correct those deviations.

Step 5 = Raise the standard, if possible, by identifying a new standard.

And what happens after step 5? The process begins again at Step 2 and is repeated over and over. In fact, that's why it's call Kaizen, continuous improvement.

Better, Because Of You

Imagine walking into a room for any reason at all, and making sure that when you leave, the room is somehow better than it was when you arrived. Maybe that means straightening a pile of papers, picking a piece of trash off the floor, or finding something that shouldn't be there and taking it back to where it belongs.

When you get a file out of a cabinet, could you leave the drawer better than it was when you came to it? Perhaps by tossing material that's outdated, replacing a torn folder, or correcting something that was previously misfiled? When you put an item back on a shelf, could you straighten the items around it?

Even just saying a kind word to someone when you walk through a room leaves that room better than it was before. The possibilities are endless.

Suppose you and everyone you know personally and at work always made sure that whatever they encountered was better when they left it than when they got to it. Wow! That would make a difference.

The Third Question

Taking an interest in other people is a lost art. Our society teaches us to focus on "me." We need to learn how to think outside ourselves. One extremely important lesson in that direction is what I call "The Third Question."

When speaking with someone, try to get to at least three questions. Most people ask a question, then move to another topic or turn the conversation to themselves. It goes like this:

Person A: *What did you do this weekend?*

Person B: *I went to the beach.*

Person A: *I went to the park and it was very hot there, but we took a cooler and the kids played on the swings and we threw a ball around and had a great time.*

Imagine how much more connected and valued Person B would feel if Person A instead asked at least three questions.

Person A: *What did you do this weekend?*

Person B: *I went to the beach.*

Person A: *That sounds great. Which beach?*

Person B: *Fort Lauderdale beach.*

Person A: *Did you actually go into the water, or was it too cold?*

Etc.

There's nothing magical about the number of questions being three. It's just a guide, and something to lodge in our memories. There are times when many more questions are appropriate.

By intentionally making The Third Question part of who you are, you will become a person who expresses true interest in others. As word gets out, you will be surrounded with people who love to speak to you, because your friendship will be to them like a cup of cold water in the desert.

Dump Your Stress

It's no fun being stressed out. A sense of despair rushes in. Getting caught up seems impossible. The world looks gray and bleak. Fortunately a simple technique can often break this cycle and put us back on track. I call it the Mind Dump.

Stress and overwhelm live on the right side of the brain. Right brain thinking can be wonderful. It allows us to create and appreciate art, nature, music, and so many joyous elements of life. It's also where our emotions reside, which can be good or bad.

During times of stress, the right brain gets overloaded. It's as though a pipeline six feet in diameter opened up and flooded the mind. The right brain has no way to deal with this other than to just feel it. Our outlook becomes nearly hopeless.

Over on the left side of the brain we have the capacity to think logically. We can analyze situations, assess them realistically, and find solutions. And since humans have enormous capacity, rarely is the left brain stumped. It can most always lead us out of the forest.

So how do we transfer our thinking from the left brain to the right? Through the Mind Dump.

Take a piece of paper and a pen (I use a small notebook designated just for this purpose) and write down everything that's bothering you. Don't try to make it pretty or use lofty words. Don't even give it much thought. Just write what comes to your head as it's coming. (Note: I do not recommend doing this on a computer as there can be too many distractions there.)

In my world a Mind Dump might look something like this:

- Bookkeeper out sick ... Is invoicing getting behind? ... Will this affect cash flow?

- I've been sneezing ... I hope I don't get sick.

- Must finish proposal on the Foster account ... When am I going to find time?

- Payment for huge bill from major supplier is due in 25 days ... Yikes!
- Traveling north next week ... Need to buy warmer clothes.
- Deadline for ROI report to client is Thursday.

Etc.

Once I have it all written down, I read it. Just this exercise often helps. That's because all of that junk is now out of the right brain where it screams for attention, and is on the left side where logic and reason kick in. If some action comes to mind for an entry, I'll write it down or implement it immediately. If not, I'll go back to my normal routine. I probably won't feel completely better, but things are starting to look up.

And then the magic happens. Because these situations are now in the left brain, analysis, logic, reasoning, etc. take place. Plans, next steps and whole solutions begin to surface. I feel more positive. The light is chasing away the darkness. The truth is setting me free. I am no longer living solely by my feelings, but am walking in the belief that there is hope.

The Mind Dump. Simple, yet very effective. A great weapon in the battle against stress.

Rise Above Stress With Checklists

Anyone who's spent any time in the cockpit of an airplane knows that pilots use several tools which are very low tech but essential. Checklists. There are the Preflight Checklist, the Engine Start Checklist, the Run Up, Taxi, Pre-Take Off, Climb Out, Cruise Flight, Approach and many other checklists always within the pilot's reach.

When asked why they have all these, one pilot answered "So I don't have to remember what to do, especially in stress-filled situations."

We all experience stress now and then. During those times it's easy to forget some important basics. We neglect to take the toothbrush on vacation because we were packing in a hurry. We hang up the phone and realize we didn't ask for the prospect's e-mail address. A friend's birthday comes and goes without our sending a card.

In all these cases, a simple checklist could help. They're extremely valuable to business productivity and personal development as well.

Take a lesson from a very critical and potentially stressful profession and think about what checklists might be beneficial in your unique circumstances. Your life will fly higher as a result.

The 20-Second Timeout

The 20-Second Timeout is a key element of professional football. When things are getting especially tense, one team or the other calls a 20-Second Timeout. Everyone gets together on the sideline, takes a deep breath, discusses strategy, etc. Likewise, in our jobs or our personal lives taking just 20 seconds can make a big difference.

Imagine you are getting ready to walk out the door to meet some friends and see a movie. Before you do, you stop for just 20 seconds and think "Am I forgetting anything? Is there something else I can do along the way?" You might remember that you have to mail the electric bill payment and there's a mailbox next to the movie theatre ... Or that the last time you went to that theatre it was cold, so you should bring a sweater. Twenty seconds was all it took.

Suppose you're getting ready to call a client about a proposal you sent earlier that week. You're just about to reach for the phone, but you pause first to ask yourself if there's anything else you can discuss with that client. You remember that she previously expressed interest in another product your company offers, so while you're on the phone, you bring this up as well. "Glad you mentioned that," the client says, and away you go.

Life in general sometimes gets overwhelming. Fears and concerns cloud our thinking. We barely know which way to turn or what task to tackle next. Taking just 20 seconds to clear our minds, see the big picture, and then re-evaluate can be extremely significant.

Why not take 20 seconds right now to experience how powerful this concept can be? Then make the 20-Second Timeout part of your game plan.

Fight, Flight, Or Freeze

If we fail to apply conscious thought to a situation, we are in danger of entering a state called fight, flight, or freeze. Psychologists describe this as a very primal response that is built into all humans.

Imagine a distant ancestor walking through the wilderness and being confronted by a wild animal. Many people would simply freeze in their tracks. For others, the mind goes to one of two possibilities ... fight for your life, or run for your life. There is not a lot of thinking involved.

Unfortunately, those who put projects off until the last minute, or multi-task excessively, or over analyze can also find themselves in a situation where the productive mind shuts down. They are left choosing between fight, flight, and freeze.

Freezing consists of doing nothing, avoiding the problem altogether, or pretending it doesn't exist. This is about as effective in the personal or professional life as it is in the jungle face to face with a hungry tiger. Fight might mean pulling an all nighter or doing something substandard just to get it over with. And flight may involve further procrastination or escaping into an easier project. Obviously, none are good solutions.

Leave the fight, flight, or freeze reaction back in the stone age where it belongs. Instead, be intentional with your thinking.

Steps For Facing Challenges

Here are a few strategies to help you face challenging times.

- Remain Focused.
  Ask yourself what the really important things are that need to be done, and then concentrate on them.

- Do What You Can.
  If something comes to mind that you can accomplish to lighten the workload, help others in need, or improve a situation, give it your best.

- Stay Positive.
  After you've done whatever you can, strive to maintain a positive attitude. Thinking and talking in a negative way about how hot it is will not make you or those around you feel cooler. Negativity only makes situations worse, so avoid it.

- Work Hard.
  Sometimes there's no substitute for rolling up your sleeves, putting in the hours and making the necessary efforts.

Difficulties are a fact of life. Focused hard work, performed to the best of your ability with a positive attitude will go a long way toward overcoming them.

Panic In Advance

People tell me I worry too much. And as if to further underscore what they perceive as this being a flaw in my character, they point out that most of what I worry about never comes to pass. I have a different view. My feeling is that the reason those problems don't occur is precisely because of the time I spend worrying over them.

Worry comes in a few varieties. Some people refuse to bother with it at all. They take the approach that whatever will happen will happen and they'll deal with it then. Others go for sitting stationary while wringing their hands. Lastly, there is the roll up your sleeves and look for solutions type.

Letting chips fall where they may before pondering possible responses often leads to panic and chaos. True, most situations do get handled, but stress, high blood pressure, late nights. and strained relationships are common byproducts.

Fretting just makes things worse. The problem doesn't go away, and now you also have to overcome the results of being a basket case. Since time is typically a factor in worrisome matters, wasting it by doing nothing is catastrophic.

The best option, therefore, is to look down the road, see an issue that might become problematic and begin worrying about it long before it hits. In the majority of cases you'll think of some action that can be taken to at least mitigate the negative consequences if not circumvent them altogether. If you're going to panic, it's best to do so in advance, when you have the benefit of weeks, days, or at least hours with a clear head, and when more possible routes to the desired outcome can be tried.

Be warned, however. Once you incorporate this as a habit in your life, people are likely to criticize. They'll tell you that you worry too much about things that don't come to pass. When that happens you can do what I do. Just smile and go back to your relatively peaceful life.

Three Little Words For Reducing Stress

Stress is a very real part of personal and professional life. The following principles may help overcome it.

- Back To Basics – Nothing combats stress like simplicity. Eliminate complexity and get down to what matters most.

- Overcome Big Stressors – Try to identify the most nagging, stressful projects and get them, or at least parts of them, out of your hair.

- Take Time Out – Get away from the source of the stress. Go for a walk. Sit in your car and listen to music.

- Organize Your World – Clean up your surroundings. File something.

- Discard The Clutter – Throw away and/or delete as much unnecessary stuff as you can.

- Clarify The Vision – Get a true picture of what really needs to be accomplished.

- Remove The Superfluous – Not everything HAS to be done. If there will be no negative repercussions, simply don't do some of the projects on your plate. Ever.

- Stop The Incoming – Put the phone on Do Not Disturb. Set an Auto Responder on your e-mail and don't check it. Close your door. Tell people that you're in a very important strategic session ... because you are ... with yourself.

- Utilize A Buddy – Get someone to cover for you while you're in stress reduction mode.

- Return The Ball – Look for projects and tasks that are cluttering your desk and your life that can be quickly sent back to someone else's court. Sign the check, OK the memo, provide the phone number, etc.

- Visualize The Reward – If you're going to be stressed out, you deserve a reward. It should be in line with the scope of hardships you've had to endure. Maybe it's a banana split, dinner out, a drive in the hot rod (for those who have a hot rod), a call to an old friend, or a movie. If you visualize the reward while you're going through the stress, it makes the situation a little less horrible. Be sure to give yourself the reward... don't let anything take it away.

• That's The End – At least for now.

Things work out best for the people who make the best of the way things work out.

- John Wooden

Some circumstances simply can not be controlled. They just happen. What we CAN control, however, is how we react to those circumstances.

Between any event and our response to that event there exists a space. Within that space, we are free to choose our reaction. Will we become negative? Will we find someone to blame? Or will we maintain a positive attitude while seeking a solution?

No doubt there are situations in all of our lives that we wish were different. Learning to recognize the space between stimulus and response, and then choosing the appropriate reaction, is a significant key to happiness and success.

Peaches, Capacity, And Capability

Two friends from south Florida thought they found a way to make their fortune. First, they bought a pickup truck with no money down. Then they drove to Georgia and filled the truck as much as they could – to capacity – with peaches for which they paid $1 a bag. They drove back home, set up a stand by the side of the road and sold those peaches for $1 a bag.

By the end of just one day they sold out of peaches. But when the cost of the peaches, the truck payment, gas and other expenses were deducted from what had come in from sales, they found that they had lost money. After some thought one of them declared, "Aha, I figured it out. We should have bought a bigger truck."

People chuckle at that story. Yet so many times men and women think that the solution to their problems is more – more of something. "If I just had more time, more employees, more education, more money, this problem would be solved." But maybe "more" is not the answer. Maybe greater capacity is not the key.

More employees can be good. They can also create a payroll burden that puts a company under. Education is wonderful, but knowledge by itself has limited value. And how many relationships have been ruined and character flaws revealed by the pressures of a sudden increase in net worth?

Vacations are another example. People often try to pack in just as much as they can. Later they say, "I need a vacation from my vacation!" This is a symptom of the "More is better" mindset.

The alternate approach involves focusing on capability rather than capacity. Capability asks "What tools, talents, or resources do I need? Which do I already possess and how can I develop them to make my life count?" It's not about packing more in, but about creating the right outcomes.

More isn't always the solution. A bigger truck doesn't always mean more profit. Instead, focus on meaningful results.

A Full Teacup

A Chinese proverb says "A full teacup can hold no more tea."

Sounds obvious, right? And yet many times people overlook this truth, keep the cup full of old tea, and thus deprive themselves of fresh, new tea.

A drawer full of outdated files can hold no new files. A computer folder full of projects that got postponed or canceled can hold no new, active projects. A To Do List full of tasks that never seem to get done can hold no new high-leverage opportunities.

Though not recommended, more file cabinets can be purchased and computer folders created. But clutter in the mind leaves no room for new and exciting thoughts to develop. A mind filled with thoughts, worries, and concerns can hold no new inspiration.

There are dozens of applications for this proverb – at work, at home, with family, in the personal life – pretty much everywhere.

Look around. Do you see any full teacups? If so, it would be wise to empty them a little ... and then enjoy the new tea.

The Quest For Capacity

At its simplest, capacity refers to the level of output of which an entity is capable. A one-gallon jug can pour out one gallon of liquid. That is its capacity.

For a business, the equation is more complex, drawing on the maximum utilization of labor, talent, materials, capital and other variables.

Several factors affect capacity. Procedures, for one thing, can make a difference. An organization with well thought out procedures, that follows and improves upon them, will operate more efficiently and therefore have greater capacity.

Asking the "Why" question (Why are we doing this?) affects capacity. If a team has a clear vision and its efforts are headed in the right direction it will accomplish more, which equals increased capacity.

Ability also affects capacity. When it comes to building a house, my capacity is quite limited. When it comes to conducting a business seminar, however, my capacity improves quite a bit.

No doubt companies that desire to serve their clients and make a profit must maximize capacity as much as possible. The factors described above will help make that a reality.

Productivity And The Leather Factory

Businesses and individuals place great emphasis on producing a large volume of output. But just being able to produce does not equal success. More important than how much we turn out is what we turn out.

A certain woman owned a leather factory. She went to the company's general manager and said, "I'm going on a journey to make sales of ladies' handbags. During the time I'm gone I want you to get this factory producing them, because when I return I'll have orders to fulfill."

With that the owner left on her journey. Sure enough she was successful in her sales efforts and came back with a briefcase packed with orders for ladies' handbags. Upon her return, the manager greeted her and said "I'm so excited, I have some great news. While you were gone, I devised a way to be extremely productive in the manufacture of men's wallets. As a result, I've got a whole warehouse filled with men's wallets for you."

How do you think that worked out? The manager was very productive, but the factory couldn't ship the orders that the owner brought back. They couldn't meet the needs of their customers. Great volume and output. No fulfillment.

It's critically important to see beyond just the amount that can be produced. Meeting specific needs with our efforts is the critical element. And that goes for business and our personal lives as well.

What – not just how much – will you accomplish with your life?

Clean Desk, Sick Mind?

Words on the side of the coffee mug say "A Clean Desk Is The Sign Of A Sick Mind." The people who wrote, produced and sold that should be ashamed of themselves for spreading such lies!

How many business people furnish their offices with beautiful shelves, credenzas and bookcases, only to cover them with piles of dingy files and magazines that haven't been reviewed in years? This sends a message of unprofessionalism to any boss, co-worker, or visitor, and certainly makes the person working in that office less productive.

Organization and lack of clutter are beneficial in many ways. Productivity experts say that those who are most effective keep only one project on their desks at any time – the one on which they're working right then. This creates a sense of focus that can't be achieved when there are papers all around.

And consider time lost to looking for documents and articles. Disorganization creates many wasted hours in a week. One consultant suggests replacing the phrase "filing system" with "retrieval system." It's simple to throw things in files or on stacks, but being able to retrieve them when needed is valuable beyond measure.

Untidiness also drains our enthusiasm. Clinical studies have shown that just looking at a basket full of laundry extracts as much energy as actually putting it in the washer. Remember that the next time your eyes fall on a mountain of papers that will eventually require your attention. Better to store them out of sight for handling one at a time.

It would be great if the person who wrote that coffee mug phrase could read this article. By following its advice and getting organized, he or she might have more time to enjoy the coffee.

Beyond Problems Lie Solutions

Problems are a lot more common than solutions. If you follow the news, you'll see the evidence. Likewise, listen to most people talk, and you'll likely hear more negative than positive. Left unchallenged, that mentality can easily creep into an individual or organization, making life and work more difficult.

For example, I could end this thought here. If I did, I'd be exposing a problem without giving any type of solution. What value would there be in that?

With most every problem, there is a solution. The first step toward finding that solution is having the mindset to realize it exists. It's like looking for a pen in a drawer. If you know for sure that the pen is in there, you'll keep looking until you find it. So, when you uncover a problem, don't stop. Let that be the motivation to start searching for the solution.

Pain Relievers Of The Human Kind

There was a day when a person with a headache had two choices: take aspirin or tough it out. Non-prescription pain reliever options were limited. Then came buffered aspirin, powders, pills that claimed to know right where we hurt, and more. The floodgates opened. Today there are scores of these remedies, accounting for tens of billions of dollars in sales.

Pain relief is a big deal. And that's true of consumers, family members, and companies as well as backs and foreheads.

What keeps your prospects awake nights? Why might they typically dread doing business with your industry? When they contact you or a competitor, what were the factors that got them to take action? Figure out the answers to these questions; make yourself or your company the pain reliever; get the word out; and listen to the phone ring.

The same principle applies to personal relationships. Think about the needs of your spouse, children, co-workers, and friends. Do what you can to make the symptoms of a challenging life more bearable. You'll be providing a tremendous service as you become the most sought-after person in every circle of your life.

People who need to spend money are going to select a company that understands their hurts and how to overcome them. Likewise for individuals deciding with whom to spend some free time. Those human pain relievers are simply priceless.

Be A Solutions Source

Solutions never go out of style. In business, people are always willing to pay for them. And the value of a solution is in direct proportion to the size of the problem being solved.

How do you provide solutions?

The first step is extremely simple, but frequently overlooked. Listen. Listen deeply to the customer, co-worker, friend, or your spouse. Thoroughly and carefully read their memos or e-mail if the communication is written. Don't interrupt. Don't tell them the story about yourself that came to mind while they were talking. Instead, ask questions. Try to hear what's beneath the surface. This type of connection will draw people – and business – to you like metal to a magnet. G. K. Chesterton said "A problem well defined is a problem half solved." So listen until you truly grasp and can define the problem.

Once you understand the problem, engage whatever parts of the team you need. It might be something you can do on your own. That's fine ... so apply 100% of your best efforts. If you need help from another department, by all means ask for it.

Third, stay humble. Truly successful people are learning and growing all the time. If you think you already know everything, you'll never learn anything. Instead, welcome the feedback that comes even after you present your solution. That's how you raise the bar and get better.

By following these steps you'll become known as a source for solutions. Enhanced personal and business relationships will follow.

The Solution Is "Plus"

People and companies want solutions. Certainly there are plenty of problems out there ... that's the easy part. Firms that can provide solutions to those problems will prosper in any economy. And a major key to solutions is one word: "Plus."

Plus is the difference between a commodity and a solution. For example, I take my cars to a certain shop because they fix my cars, PLUS they've proven to have my best interests in mind and to be honest. I'm not sure if their mechanics turn wrenches better than the shop down the street, but the problem of wondering if I'm being told the truth has been completely solved.

Make Plus part of your standard operating procedure by adding a Plus to what you do as often as you can.

It starts by opening your mind to the possibilities. Frequently ask yourself and members of your team, "How can we add Plus to this?" Share your Plus ideas and the times when you added Plus on your own, or caught someone else adding Plus.

An organization can have a lot of fun with this. And Plus is really good for business.

The Plus Perspective

I own a hot rod Mustang which needed new tires awhile back. As part of the process, I thought I'd take the opportunity to give the car a better look. So I stopped at a national franchise tire store, took the salesperson out to my car and had the following conversation:

Me: I need new tires for the Mustang, but I want to put bigger tires on the back than on the front, so the car has a more aggressive stance.

Salesperson: No you don't.

Me: Why not?

Salesperson: Because if you put bigger tires on the back, you'll never be able to rotate your tires and you'll wind up replacing them sooner.

Me: OK. Thank you. I'll have to think about it. (I said, not wanting to appear stupid, as I got in my car and left.)

This salesperson had it all wrong. Because he didn't listen to what I said or size me up properly by asking questions, he falsely concluded that I was interested in tires – those round rubber things that go on the wheels of a car. Big mistake. Instead, I was after a solution to what I perceived as a problem with the Mustang ... its appearance wasn't aggressive enough.

What the salesperson could have done is sold me tires, PLUS the look I was after. That's exactly what the Mustang performance shop did.

What do you or your business produce? If you think it's certain products or services, that's only half right. You supply that, PLUS something. The extra something is the solution customers really want. Find the Plus and provide it.

Remember, if you ever need a helping hand, you'll find one at the end of your arm. As you grow older you will discover that you have two hands. One for helping yourself, and the other for helping others.

- Audrey Hepburn

The pressures of life can sometimes seem overwhelming. Often, the best solution is simply to jump in and start accomplishing the tasks before us. The talents and resources we're given have tremendous potential, but only as we utilize them can we realize their positive effects.

Friends and neighbors face difficult seasons in life, too. The same personal characteristics that get us through our own hard times can, and should, be used for their benefits as well.

This day will surely bring challenges – to you and those with whom you come in contact. Much of what you need to help yourself and others is as near as your own abilities.

Adding Pop

What do you do for Pop? And no, I don't mean for your dad.

I remember the night I had dinner with a friend. I noticed that the server had on a large, shiny ring in the shape of a flower. When I commented on it, she replied "I wear this for Pop."

Of course I couldn't let that comment slide, so I asked a few questions. What I learned was that at that particular restaurant, all the servers are required to dress in a black top, shorts and shoes. In addition, they each have to add three items to their wardrobe that are brightly colored. These are called Pop.

Looking around, I noticed pink suspenders, orange socks, yellow headbands and the like. My new friend, Brooke, sported the ring plus a peach colored undershirt and knee-highs.

So what do you and I do for Pop? How do we add color and brightness to performing our jobs, living our individual lives, interfacing with clients, co-workers, family, and friends? What little extras can we do that just might spice up all of our interactions and output?

Here's the place where I would usually insert some examples. But instead of that, I'll leave it up to you to think of ways to create Pop. You might even want to get together with someone and discuss it. Maybe over a meal at a certain restaurant where the servers really know how to dress.

Great Expectations

A phrase that businesses often use when they talk about customer service is "exceeding expectations." They say things like "We want to exceed your expectations." That sounds nice, but what does it really mean?

Customers have expectations about how businesses should treat them. We expect cashiers to act a certain way, salespeople to act a certain way, waiters and waitresses to act a certain way, etc. Exceeding expectations means that those people act better than we expected them to act.

Exceeding expectations involves performing in ways that are above and beyond. You have to answer customers' questions more thoroughly than they expected, solve their problems more completely and quickly than they expected, provide services that they didn't expect you to provide, and more.

Think about your industry and what you can do, specifically, to exceed customer's expectations. Then do it.

Speak Reasonable, Act Remarkable

To exceed your customers' expectations, you must first be sure that the expectations are reasonable to begin with. "Reasonable" is the key word. You don't want your customers' expectations to be too high or too low.

Often, we set others' expectations ourselves. So when a customer asks how long something will take, you should answer honestly. If you know something will take three hours, you should not say "I can have that done in an hour" just to get the order. By doing so, you set up a scenario where you will disappoint your customer, make yourself look bad, and jeopardize the relationship. On the other hand, you should not say "That will take five hours." Your customer may have an idea of how long the request should take, and by padding the expectations you risk appearing unprofessional.

Instead, give an honest answer, thus setting reasonable expectations. In the example above, you would tell the customer that it should take three hours. That becomes the customer's expectation. Then, you should do everything in your power to exceed that expectation by completing the request sooner than you said, or by making it better than the customer expected in the same amount of time, or by showing more than one version of the project, etc.

Set reasonable expectations. Then exceed them.

Winning The Wow!

Question: How do you know when you've exceeded your customers' expectations?

Answer: Wow!

When you exceed someone's expectations, the natural response is for that person to say or think "Wow!" The "Wow!" is automatic and spontaneous.

There have been times when I've assigned a project to someone, and it's come back to me so quickly that I've said "Wow!" Other times I've listened to someone's innovative idea, or read an e-mail or memo, and "Wow!" has come to mind.

Go for the "Wow!" as often as you can. It's a reliable indication that you're exceeding expectations.

To Come Out Ahead, Put Others First

Johnny Carson, who hosted The Tonight Show from 1962 to 1992 once had Conrad Hilton, founder of the Hilton Hotels & Resorts chain, on as a guest. Carson asked Mr. Hilton to reflect on his long, prosperous career and provide a message to the American people. After some thought, Hilton turned to the camera and said, "Please put the shower curtain inside the tub."

Isn't that human nature? So often, my thoughts are only about what is good for me. Carson, and the viewing audience no doubt, wanted to receive advice that would contribute to their lives. Hilton saw an opportunity to benefit himself, creating less work for his staff and the need for fewer maintenance problems in his properties.

In business, personal relationships, and life in general, those who put others' interests before their own most often come out ahead. Companies that are customer-focused get our loyalty. People who seek win-win solutions to complex situations establish more alliances than those with a my way or the highway attitude.

The apostle Paul wrote "Look out not only to your own interests, but also for the interests of others." That's a good maxim to follow. And if there had been Hilton Hotels in Paul's day, it's likely that he would never have left a pool of water on the bathroom floor.

Did I Say That?

There's a game often played at parties, where participants are not allowed to say a specific word or they'll lose some prize. If that game were played and people weren't allowed to say the word "I", they'd be shocked at how often it's used.

When friends, coworkers, and even customers and vendors talk about their weekend or their problems, will you dig deeper and ask follow-up questions? Or will you reach for the trusty "I" and reply "I did this over the weekend", or "I have this problem in my life."?

Personal relationships work best when each party is given equal time. If either person uses more than his or her share of "I", which is often the case, the friendship becomes one-sided and stagnant. In the business world, when dealing with customers, the ratio should be even more dramatic, with providers of products and services doing the majority of listening and asking clarifying questions rather than saying "I."

It's impossible to avoid saying "I" altogether. But most of us can certainly use it much less than we do. Start listening for the "I"s you say.

So there you have it. A method to become better at staying focused on other people. And an essay in which I've managed not to refer to myself with the word "I" until this very last sentence.

Forming Your Reputation

A good reputation is extremely valuable. It generates positive results with clients, vendors, fellow team members, family, friends. Just about everybody.

How does a person or a company develop and maintain a good reputation? It starts with the first impression and then builds by what is done consistently.

Favorable first impressions can come from a business' logo, corporate ID materials, web site, the way people answer the phone, the friendliness, appearance and busy-ness of the team when visitors or customers are present, the neatness of work spaces, and more. Individuals make first impressions in other ways.

After the first impression, consistency determines the reputation. If people in a company acknowledge every e-mail, produce accurate work time and again, pay bills within terms, cooperate pleasantly with fellow team members, etc. – or if they don't – they earn the corresponding reputation. The results will follow suit as well. For example, if the staff always returns voice messages promptly, clients won't be frustrated by the need to leave a message.

First impression plus consistency equals reputation. Reputations bring corresponding consequences. Maintaining a superb reputation and building on it will pay off handsomely in many ways.

The Value Of Reputation

The wisest man who ever lived said "A good name is rather to be chosen than great riches."

Having a solid reputation is an asset in virtually every business or personal scenario. My advertising agency once discovered that we had overcharged a client several thousand dollars. When we informed the client, she could have thought we had tried to pull one over on her. But that never crossed her mind. Why? Because we have a reputation of integrity.

Once in awhile we have to tell a client that a deadline is humanly impossible. They believe us. Why? Because we have a reputation for doing whatever IS humanly possible.

A good reputation can help companies get credit from vendors, price breaks from suppliers, and repeat business from clients. Individuals with stellar reputations are sought after as friends, get promotions, and become mentors.

No person or business can rest on a reputation and get slack. Instead, they have to keep building on what they've already established. No doubt there will be times in the future when that consistent positive reputation will be an important asset. That's the value of reputation.

Reputation Maintenance

Reputations come in many flavors, from very good to very bad. Once they are built, they are maintained by consistent action.

A first class reputation can't be maintained with mediocre actions. Instead, stellar actions are the only way to maintain stellar reputations. In fact, the bar continues to rise. A business colleague of mine acknowledges all his e-mails within moments of their receipt when he's in the office, and sets up an auto-responder when he's out. Clients know that. It's his reputation. One time when he was delayed and not able to reply to e-mail for a couple hours, clients called asking if everything was OK. They've come to expect certain actions, based on reputation.

An even greater concern is the possibility of losing a top reputation. Actions that are contrary to the reputation that's been established can do that. Nobody's perfect, so how can one hope to keep an excellent reputation? It's usually not the mistake, but what comes AFTER it that determines reputation.

An attitude of apathy, finger pointing, and slow response will hurt a person's or company's reputation more than the mistake itself. An attitude of intense concern, acceptance of responsibility, and immediate over-and-above resolution can do more good for a reputation than the damage caused by the error. Of course a company or person that consistently makes mistakes will get a reputation as a mistake-maker. That must be avoided.

Improving a damaged reputation takes consistent performance that is always better than what's been done in the past. And it can take a very long time. Some people are more generous than others in handing out forgiveness, but still, it's very tough to repair a tarnished reputation, though it can be done.

Reputations. They're extremely valuable. Those who build rock-solid ones and work to maintain them deserve all the long-term success that will surely come their way.

Of all the things you wear, your expression is the most important.

- Janet Lane

Psychologists call it body language, and it's as easy to read as a book. Our facial expression can tell the world whether we're confident or nervous during a meeting, if we feel successful or not in our current situation, and whether our outlook for the future is positive or negative.

Fortunately, we can control our expression. A little thought about those things for which we are thankful will often change our inner attitude and our outward demeanor as well. A cheerful expression helps us look our best, which in turn makes us more likely to be well received by others.

Society places great emphasis on the outward appearance. We respond accordingly by selecting clothes, watches, jewelry, etc. that reflect the type of image we want to portray. It's easy to forget, however, that our expression says more about us than anything else we wear.

Life Management Buzz Words

The world of life management contains a maze of buzz words. There are goals, objectives, mission, vision, purpose, values, strategies, passion, tactics, and many others. Add "core", "authentic", or "central" before any of those and you'll create a whole new crop of phrases. It's downright confusing.

Rather than get bogged down in the terminology, it's best to understand the process. Life management starts at a high level and works downward. And the easiest way to make sense of the buzz words is to see them in the same way.

Level = Highest. In the clouds. Words = Mission, Values, Vision, Purpose, Passion.

These words help answer the question "Why was I put here on Earth?" or similar. A typical application would be "Consider your core values, then write a statement defining your central mission for your life." (Substitute other buzz words in the list, and the application stays the same.)

Level = Closer to the ground. Words = Objective, Strategy, Vision

The person is now identifying issues that are important to him or her, though not yet considering any specific steps to be taken. For example, an objective (or strategy or vision) might be "I want to improve professionally," or "My brother knows I love him," or "I am 15 pounds lighter."

Level = We've landed. Words = Goals, Roles

Goals take objectives and make them tangible and measurable. They are often stated within a person's specific role. For the objective above – I want to improve professionally, which falls into the person's career role – there could be several goals, such as "I will take three online courses this year", "I will volunteer to help my boss with a project over and above my normal duties," and "I will find someone who has already reached a higher professional level than myself and ask that person to mentor me."

Level = On the surface. Words = Tasks, Tactics, Next Steps

Tactics are the actual steps that lead toward accomplishing the goal. They can be as small as looking up a phone number, or as large as writing a report that could take weeks or even months. Tactics are where the actual efforts occur. These are often broken down into sub tasks.

The next time you hear or read about core values leading to strategic goal setting within specific roles that result in tactical components designed to fulfill a key vision, you'll be right there with full understanding. At least that was my objective.

Life Management, Step One

Life management is the practice of a person looking at how he or she lives. It of course involves time management, because how we spend our time is how we spend our life. But life management goes beyond the mere "how" questions and looks into the "who" and "why".

The first step in life management is to become intimately connected with the deepest part of your being. Later, decisions about the way you manage time and other resources will flow from this understanding of who you are and why you feel you exist.

Stephen Covey, in his book *The 7 Habits Of Highly Effective People*, brought this concept to the masses by teaching about the personal mission statement. Other personal development gurus are likewise on board, promoting vision statements, core values, personal DNA, purpose statements, etc. These are all very similar to one another.

To embark on a life management process, start by writing a paragraph, a sentence or two, or maybe a series of bullet points that answers the question "Why was I put here on Earth?" It's that simple … and that complex.

Regardless of what you call it, this statement is mandatory for a true journey into life management. I encourage you to take some time and accomplish it.

MBO For Life

Peter Drucker (1909-2005) has been called "the man who invented management." His books are classics and form the basis for a great deal of what business leaders after him taught. One of Drucker's philosophies is called "Management By Objective", or MBO.

MBO is just as it sounds: managing in such a way as to achieve a pre-defined objective. When Drucker taught this in the 1960s, he was referring to businesses, assembly lines, and the like. Later, along came Stephen Covey and others who applied MBO to personal development. With that, the concept of life management was born.

To look at your life from an MBO perspective means that you start with a high level view. You envision yourself flying over your ideal future at 30,000 feet, and as you look down, you record what you see. It's all part of getting in touch with your core. That becomes your ultimate objective, which you will later break down into smaller objectives.

You then manage your life toward accomplishing those objectives.

The opposite of MBO is Management By Crisis – MBC. Many people live in MBC mode. For example, they may have an objective to keep their car maintained, but they don't manage to that objective (MBO.) Then one day the crisis comes – a serious mechanical problem that leaves them stranded; so they have no choice but to manage to that: MBC. This plays out in other ways involving health, relationships, financial decisions, etc.

Get in touch with your core. Define your high level objectives. And engage an MBO lifestyle as you manage toward those objectives. You'll then be on your way to effective life management.

Who Am I?

A key step in mastering life management involves answering a question about yourself. That question is "Who am I?" Think about the roles you fill, and the fact that you are significant to so many others. One person can be a daughter, a mother, a sister, a wife, a professional, a friend, a neighbor, a volunteer, etc. The number of lives that are touched is huge.

One "Who am I?" role that is often forgotten is that "I am a person." The command to "Love your neighbor as yourself" indicates that we must love ourselves. We need to discover what energizes us, physically, spiritually and mentally / emotionally, and then give ourselves permission to experience those things.

Identifying your roles in life is a powerful life management component. Embrace who you are as a unique individual and find the joy in playing that part.

The Butterfly Effect

In December 1972, meteorologist Edward Lorenz presented a revolutionary talk to the American Association for the Advancement of Science in Washington, D.C. His title was *Predictability: Does the Flap of a Butterfly's Wings in Brazil Set Off a Tornado in Texas?* Lorenz concluded that when one condition changes – no matter how simply – a mathematical chain of events begins, the end of which can be enormous.

Business people and astute students of life in general are keenly aware of the truth of what has become known as The Butterfly Effect. Each day those individuals make proactive moves that set plans in motion. They watch for the results, then evaluate and adjust in an effort to draw closer to their goals.

The Butterfly Effect is also a reminder that very small efforts can eventually bring great rewards. Even modest marketing budgets, properly executed, may return profits which can be reinvested to ultimately create a large company. Lengthy novels, written one page at a time, become best sellers, screenplays, and movies. Seemingly small kindnesses makes a huge difference in the lives of those who long for the warmth of a friend. And what may be perceived as a drop in the bucket of personal development can wind up becoming a life-changing habit down the road.

Perhaps Edward Lorenz shocked the scientific world, but he didn't surprise those who live each day with their eyes open. Such people know that what they do today has a profound effect on many tomorrows.

Seeing Life From A Hot Air Balloon

Every human development expert agrees that setting goals is a major factor in determining whether or not a person will realize his or her full potential. Goal setting is extremely valuable for businesses, careers, personal lives, relationships, and overall growth. There are a few techniques and pointers that may be beneficial.

The first step in setting goals is not about goals at all. It's about determining why you feel you were placed here on Earth, through what is sometimes called the Life Mission Statement. This is a simple phrase that describes your core purpose. It doesn't have to be eloquent or creative, though it will be highly meaningful.

A popular and helpful next step in goal setting is the imaginary hot air balloon ride.

Imagine yourself in a hot air balloon. As you look down, you see your life as you'd like it to be at some point in the future. Are you exercising more? Playing golf or tennis? Learning something new? Are there personality traits in your future self that have not yet been built into your character? Where are you professionally? Have you learned new skills? Taken on more responsibility?

Now, write down as much as you can from the imaginary hot air balloon ride.

Commit yourself to making this vision a reality. The next season of life will be much more profitable than it would have been otherwise.

Life In The Margin

The word "Margin" has many definitions. In the context of personal development it describes a condition where someone functions at an effective level without maxing out his or her time, energy, money, patience, capacity, etc.

A person operating with little or no margin is constantly drained. A person operating with sufficient margin finds him/herself with resources left over, even after being highly productive. Operating without margin makes one ineffective in the short term, and in the long term will cause total burnout, just as running a machine at full throttle for an extended period will cause a malfunction.

When you're always racing to get somewhere at the last minute, or consistently arrive late, that's living without margin. The person who gets there early and can relax or read a magazine while waiting for the appointed time is living with margin.

If someone can afford the luxury model, but goes for the less expensive one instead, that's margin. To buy something that's going to make you late on the payment each month is to go without margin.

Eating the last slice of pizza when you're already full vs. pushing the plate away when there's still a few more French fries on it (or skipping the fries altogether in favor of the steamed vegetables) … No margin / margin. You get the idea.

Make living with margin part of your life management strategy for growth. Peace and greater productivity, rather than excess anxiety and diminished effectiveness, will result.

Living From The Top Down

Life management is a powerful growth strategy. It means looking at your life from the top down, with a big picture perspective. It involves seeing your life as a whole and coordinating who you are, what you think, what you do, etc. to lead to a desired destination.

People who are managing their lives have a clear understanding of why they were placed on Earth. The life manager arrives at this by writing a statement that gets in touch with the core of his or her being. This statement forms the basis for steps to come.

A few written sentences that describe our purpose helps us next determine several objectives for our lives. We will then manage by those objectives, measuring what we do according to them.

Life management includes identifying the many significant roles that a person fulfills. One human being can be a husband, father, son, brother, co-worker, neighbor, volunteer, friend, and more. And remember, you are first of all a person, responsible for your own well being, spiritually, physically, and mentally / emotionally.

Because demands on resources (time, money, physical capacity, etc.) are numerous, we can easily max out. When that happens, we're no good for anything. A major way to avoid this is to have margin in our lives. This means living so that there are resources left when the commitment is achieved.

The life manager looks upon all the demands and choices of life, and – like anyone else – the question "What should I do?" enters his or her mind. But this person has a roadmap. Other questions come into play, such as "Is this in line with my purpose and core values?", "Does it move me toward my objectives?", "Is this consistent with the roles that reflect my significance to others?", "If I take this on, will I maintain margin?" Based on these criteria, we move forward … or we don't.

Wake Up Call

The runner's alarm went off at 4:30 A.M. That's about the latest he could get up to do a workout and still make it to the office on time. He didn't feel like rolling out of bed and running several miles in the heat and humidity, but he knew he didn't have a choice. Why not? It's simple.

Part of his written life mission statement talks about continual improvement. One of his written values has to do with staying fit. He has a written vision to run a marathon in a certain time one day, so he established a specific written goal for his next marathon, a few months away. He follows a 20-week plan for getting there, which was well underway on the morning in question. Of course, no progress would have been made toward any of those if he had simply gone back to sleep that day.

So when the buzzer rang at 4:30 A.M. he didn't have to make a decision. It had already been made.

One of the benefits of life management is that it gives a clear roadmap for so many situations. If something aligns with our mission, values, vision, roles, goals, etc., there's strong support for doing it. If not, it's much easier to say "No" with conviction.

Thirty minutes later, dressed and ready to go, the runner hit the streets with a strong sense of purpose. It was the start of a great day.

The starting point of all achievement is desire. Keep this constantly in mind. Weak desire brings weak results, just as a small amount of fire makes a small amount of heat.

- Napoleon Hill

Desires reveal gaps in our lives that cry out to be filled. These yearnings can be uncomfortable, even unpleasant. Many try to eliminate those negative feelings. They do this by attempting to subdue the desires themselves.

Successful people, however, know that desires can be a powerful positive force, pushing us toward the accomplishment of our goals. Those people feed their desires. They envision themselves obtaining the possession, arriving at the position in life, or changing their circumstances in some specific way. The longings intensify, and so do the efforts that move those people in the corresponding direction.

What Napoleon Hill said is true: "Weak desire brings weak results." Likewise, strong desires bring strong results. What do you strongly desire today?

Vision Test

Having a vision means getting a clear picture in your mind of what you want to accomplish. If the goal is to learn a language, then it means vividly imagining yourself speaking fluently in that language. The vision could be wearing a certain size dress or pants, being involved in a specific type of relationship, mastering a skill, having a certain character trait, etc.

A vision involves seeing yourself achieving a particular goal in your mind's eye. Experts say that if you can't envision the successful accomplishment of a goal, then the goal is too lofty and will never come to fruition. It's important, therefore, to give every goal the vision test.

Studies show that the more we envision ourselves meeting our goals, the more likely we are to get there in reality. Some people use photos, note cards, and messages (sometimes cryptic) posted conspicuously to keep their goals in front of them at all times.

Whatever it takes to help you see yourself at the finish line is powerful. The key is to get a picture in your mind of you – with the goal achieved. That's vision.

What You See Is What You Get

The New York City Marathon is a 26.2 mile race that winds through all five New York burroughs. It is one of the most prestigious events in which a serious runner can compete. Something fascinating happened shortly after the finish of this race in 2009.

The winner, Meb Keflezighi, was seen on camera crying uncontrollably right after he broke the ribbon. His sobbing lasted quite awhile. When the television crew could finally interview him, they asked, "What caused you to display such emotion?" Meb's answer was, "I have visualized this for so many years, and to finally accomplish it is overwhelming."

Visualization is one of the great secrets of successful people. Athletes, business men and women, entertainers – you name it – all know and teach that a huge key to accomplishing a goal is to imagine in your mind the completion of that goal. The more accurately and vividly the mental image can be, the better. It's a technique that helps top producers in all areas of life.

To quote the timeless wisdom of King Solomon, "As a man thinks in his heart, so is he." (That goes for women, as well.) Use the gift of visualization to benefit every part of your life.

In Praise Of Goals

Successful people have goals. There is virtually no exception. What's more, these people write their goals, keep them top of mind, and use them as a road map for life. Here is what some of these highly effective people said about goals:

- *"Set your goals high, and don't stop till you get there."* - Bo Jackson, sports legend

- *"If we make up our mind what we are going to make of our lives, then work hard toward that goal, we never lose – somehow we win out."* - Ronald Reagan, 40th President of the United States

- *"Goals determine what you're going to be."* - Julius "Dr. J" Erving, NBA basketball great

- *"Setting goals is the first step in turning the invisible into the visible."* - Anthony Robbins, world-class motivational speaker

- *"We must have a theme, a goal, a purpose in our lives. If you don't know where you're aiming, you don't have a goal."* - Mary Kay Ash, founder of Mary Kay Cosmetics

- *"Unless you have definite, precise, clearly set goals, you are not going to realize the maximum potential that lies within you."* - Zig Ziglar, motivational speaker

- *"A goal is a dream with a deadline."* - Napoleon Hill, classic self-help speaker and author

- *"People with clear, written goals accomplish far more in a shorter period of time than people without them could ever imagine."* - Brian Tracy, self-help author and speaker, and consultant to Olympic athletes

Top performers believe in the power of goals. Taking the time to put yours in place is like writing chapter one of your personal success story.

No Goal, No Gain

Below is the text of an actual e-mail that I received from someone applying for a job.

Please accept this letter in application for one of the following positions within your company: Account Executive, Loan Originator, Account Manager, Office Support Staff, Branch Manager, Office Manager, Supervisor, HR Support Staff.

It's hard to achieve your goal when you don't know what it is. On the other hand, define your goals, focus on them, keep them in mind constantly, and you have a much better chance of accomplishing those goals.

I wonder if the person who sent the e-mail above ever got his dream job. I'm not sure, and chances are he's not sure either. It's important to make your goals specific.

Voices Of Success

Just in case you're not yet convinced of the power of goals, below are a few more quotes from people who have risen to the top of their fields. As you'll see, goals were a big part of their success.

- *"Choosing a goal and sticking to it changes everything."* - Scott Reed, Australian rules football star

- *"A man has to have goals – for a day, for a lifetime."* - Ted Williams, baseball legend

- *"A man without a goal is like a ship without a rudder."* - Thomas Carlyle, Scottish writer

- *"A person should set his goals as early as he can and devote all his energy and talent to getting there."* - Walt Disney, founder of the Disney empire

- *"If you go to work on your goals, your goals will go to work on you."* - Jim Rohn, rags to riches entrepreneur

- *"All who have accomplished great things have had a great aim, have fixed their gaze on a goal"* - Orison Sweet Marden, author

- *"What keeps me going is goals."* - Muhammad Ali, world Champion boxer

We can all take a lesson from these great men and women as we get serious about goals.

The chief danger in life is that you may take too many precautions.

- Alfred Adler

Most of us know the safe path all too well. From our childhoods we were told to watch out, be careful, slow down. Later, we found ourselves in daily routines. Safe, yes – but lacking excitement.

While life and limb are certainly worth protecting, some calculated risks in business, relationships, or daily activities can add vitality to our existence. Stepping out into unknown territories, trying something new, stretching what you thought were your limitations … these are the building blocks of enthusiasm!

Being cautious may be the most dangerous thing we can do. We may miss out on the thrill of living. And what a tragedy that would be.

The Accountability Alliance

One technique that can be very helpful when pursuing a goal is the element of accountability to another person. Somehow this concept has gotten a bad reputation. People think it will rob them of their free will and independence. But that's not what accountability means at all.

Accountability is about giving a human being you trust to have your best interests in mind permission to ask the hard questions about how you're doing. That person will then make suggestions, cheer the victories, and offer encouragement through the challenges. He or she will be a sounding board and an external conscience, especially when your internal will power is not quite strong enough to keep you working as hard as necessary.

Achievement experts agree that this is a major factor, whether the goal is to master a new skill, overcome a bad habit, build a particular character trait, etc. Consider these words, written hundreds of years ago by King Solomon, the wisest man who ever lived: *"Two are better than one because they have a good reward for their efforts. For if either falls, his companion can lift him up; but pity the one who falls without another to lift him up."*

Such a valuable relationship doesn't just happen. It has to be sought and intentionally set in motion. After writing a goal, it's good to consider who may have gone through a similar process, then approach him or her with a request to check your progress on a regular basis and provide input. If both parties can help each other simultaneously, the alliance is even more beneficial.

Far from heavy handedness or manipulation by guilt and intimidation, accountability creates a scenario where one person's strengths are multiplied by those of another. The partnership becomes an additional building block in the structure of success.

The Goals Behind The Goals

Most meaningful goals must be broken down into small pieces in order to be accomplished. That's because the overall objective itself is too complex to tackle all at once.

Someone who wants to become fluent in a foreign language within two years will have many steps to complete along the way. He or she may wish to research learning methods, speak to others who have mastered the language, adjust schedules in order to attend class and do homework, then identify a series of events that indicate progress.

Each element can be called a sub goal.

Sub goals are also valuable in that our minds accept their feasibility more readily than one huge undertaking. Scheduling an informative tour of the local community college, along with meeting the Spanish language professor is much easier to envision than carrying on an hour long native-tongue conversation with a citizen of Madrid.

Like mile markers on a long highway, sub goals – passed one at a time – can take us to faraway destinations.

Good Moves In Pursuit Of Goals

Virtually all effective people set goals. Of course, even more important than setting goals is accomplishing them. There are many great techniques for this. Here are a few:

- Break down your goal into small steps. Ask yourself "What is the very next step I could take toward the accomplishment of this goal?"

- Share your goal with another person. Allow him or her to check your progress on a regular basis.

- Impose a negative consequence on yourself if your goal is not reached. If your goal is to drink 64 ounces of water a day, tell yourself that you're not allowed to watch a favorite TV show that night if you don't drink the water.

- Give yourself a reward for meeting your goal. If you want to cut down on calories, it may be a bit too ambitious to think you're never going to eat sweets again. So reward yourself with one reasonable portion of ice cream on Sunday night if you forego those big bowls throughout the week.

- Talk to others who have successfully achieved a similar goal. Learn their secrets and emulate their behavior.

- Form a buddy system with someone who is trying to accomplish a similar goal. A little friendly competition can be a great motivator.

These are just a few quick pointers. I hope you find them helpful as you work toward goals of your own.

Know The Route, Reach The Goal

Achieving a goal is a wonderful thing. But the real value comes from the steps we take to make it happen and what we learn along the way. The journey follows a well-marked course.

- Set a specific goal.
- Put that goal in writing.
- Create a stretch goal (a goal that goes beyond the original goal) and write that one down as well.
- Put the spotlight on your stretch goal.
- Keep all your goals believable.
- Monitor progress, realizing that small steps will get you to the finish line.
- Celebrate every short-term victory and vow to improve every shortfall.
- Continually challenge yourself to hit new heights.
- Remain focused.
- Visualize success.
- Recognize the value of every element that contributes to progress.
- When you reach the goal, raise the bar and set a new goal and a new stretch goal.

Follow this list to set and achieve your goals.

Taking Goals To Task

The most granular element of the life management process is called a task. A task is something that can be done by applying effort to a single undertaking at a defined point in time. Tasks are critical factors of personal and organizational development, and they're sometimes very difficult.

Building a house is a huge goal. It will no doubt require many sub goals, such as: laying the foundation; erecting exterior walls; adding a roof; framing the inside; installing plumbing, electrical, and fixtures; putting up drywall and trim; and painting. Some of these sub goals may themselves have further sub goals. Eventually, however, the project will consist of a series of tasks.

The worker responsible for the foundation, for example, may decide to dig a footer on a certain day. That becomes a task. Likewise for adding steel reinforcements, pouring the concrete, and whatever else is involved in building the groundwork of a residence.

On a smaller scale, tasks may include activities such as looking up a telephone number, making a call, having lunch with someone to solicit advice, writing a memo, etc. The examples for both personal life and business are endless.

Indeed, tasks themselves are nearly unlimited, or so they seem. The truth is that by scheduling and completing tasks one at a time, layers of sub goals, then large goals themselves, are eventually accomplished.

Even the woodpecker owes his success to the fact that he uses his head and keeps pecking away until he finishes the job he starts.
- Coleman Cox

The ability to persevere is a very important factor in creating success and happiness. Everyone has opportunity. We all have areas of expertise. Each of us has been given talents. But observation reveals that those who simply stick to the task, making steady progress, emerge victorious in the long run.

Small steps toward our goals may not seem exciting when viewed individually. But the accumulation of those contributions can add up to amazing results. We look back and realize that tremendous progress was made.

Don't lose heart. Persevere to the completion of your goal. The greatest symphonies were written one note at a time.

To Plan Or Not To Plan

The lyrics to John Lennon's song "Beautiful Boy (Darling Boy)" include the famous phrase "Life is what happens to you when you're busy making other plans." As mystical and tragic as this seems, there's an even more tragic and profound truth: Life is what happens to you when you're busy NOT making other plans.

Each of us is given 24 hours in a day, seven days in a week, 365 days in a year, and an unknown number of years in our lives. That time will pass whether we manage it intentionally or not. If such a realization is alarming, the antidote may be to reach for a calendar.

Plans give goals a much better chance at becoming reality by plotting the steps necessary to achieve each goal on an actual schedule. Knowing exactly what needs to be done next and by when prompts us to use our days accordingly. If we apply the necessary discipline and execute wisely, the small pieces of the puzzle come together and the goals are accomplished.

Not making plans generally results in a life spent aimlessly wandering. Planning, however, can be the vehicle to great achievement and fulfillment. Imagine that.

Adjusting Plans

When pursuing a goal, sometimes plans have to be adjusted along the way. These mid-course modifications are done to take advantage of favorable conditions or to meet new challenges. The original goal is always kept in sight and the plan is only altered to help meet that goal.

This principle works for many areas of life. For example, if a person wants to have an extra $2500 in the bank in a year, that's approximately $50 per week. If one week he or she works overtime and gets an extra $25, it would be better to put that money in the bank than to spend it on something frivolous. After all, next week his or her sunglasses might break and s/he'd have to buy new ones. Of course there are many other areas of life where this concept applies.

When things are going well, make the most of it. The day of adversity will come, and you'll need those extra resources. The good news is that you'll have them.

Set A Date, Reach A Goal

In the life management process, the element that comes after setting goals is making plans. Plans are easy to explain and understand. They're as simple as this: dates on a calendar.

Well-defined goals break down into a series of next steps that must be taken for the goals to be accomplished. Plans, then, move those next steps to a calendar. The result is a vivid, detailed picture of when each part must be completed in order to fulfill the goal.

Using this method, virtually any goal, no matter how large, can be accomplished.

Let's suppose, for example, that someone wants to run a marathon. Next steps (which can be thought of as sub goals) might include looking up the telephone number of the running store, calling the store to find out its hours, going there and buying a pair of running shoes, reading a book on proper running form and nutrition, setting out on a few half-mile runs, then some one-mile runs, etc. until the desired 26.2 miles can be achieved. Along the way, the person might want to join a running club, buy additional gear, enter a few shorter distance events, and so forth.

Once these steps are identified, it's time to begin scheduling. The big goal is completing the marathon, so that's written on the calendar first. Then each sub goal is plotted, from the current date on. When that's done, voila! ... a plan has been created.

Planning is vital for successful life management. And though it's not always easy, it's certainly not complex. It requires nothing more than some deep thought and a calendar.

Mental Realism

There is an enormous mental element to success. In order for a goal to be achieved or a plan to be executed, the person must totally believe that the goal or plan is possible. Otherwise, the mind will almost always sabotage any efforts. This is not to say that believable goals and plans are easy, but those that are not believable are nearly impossible.

When writing goals and plotting next steps on a calendar, therefore, it's prudent to ask "Can I truly envision myself accomplishing or executing this?" A certain amount of fear or even slight doubt is normal. But if the outcome feels completely out of reach, it's best to scale back.

Someone who wants to write a novel in her spare time while juggling work and a family should not set a goal to complete the book in one week. Planning to conceive, pen and edit thirty or forty pages a day is just unrealistic. The mind will rebel to a degree that no amount of willpower can overcome.

If, on the other hand, the same woman gives herself ten months then breaks the goal of writing a novel down into next steps and plots them on a calendar, she will very likely do what few people have ever accomplished – become an author. The mental part becomes an ally instead of an enemy, pulling her toward the desired result.

Goals and plans need to pass the test of mental realism. Once they do, great things are possible.

If you don't know where you are going, how can you expect to get there?

- Basil S. Walsh

Imagine you are about to take a trip. The car is packed, the kids are buckled in, and you're ready to go. You pull out of the driveway and head down the road. But the destination of this trip was never planned, so you drive around aimlessly for days.

While it might sound ludicrous, many people treat their very lives just that haphazardly. Each day is full of activity and busy-ness, but the sense of accomplishment and fulfillment is missing. Why? Because even as the commotion began, there was no knowledge of what would constitute success.

An important first step in reaching our desired destination is determining what that destination will be. And the more specific we can make it, the better.

Decide where you want this journey of life to take you. Then when you get there, you can enjoy the satisfaction of knowing you accomplished your objective.

Make Priorities A Priority

It is very common for a person to have scores of tasks on his or her to do list. How can anyone hope to complete so many next steps in pursuit of accomplishing goals? The solution is prioritizing, a critical part of the life management process.

Those who desire to achieve great things must first realize that it's impossible to do them all at the same time. Once that reality sets in, a careful look at the big picture is in order. This means making a quick scan of all the items in one's court, and determining which are most important.

Generally, numbering every task in its priority order is unwieldy. Many experts, therefore, suggest assigning an A, B, or C to each item, then coming back and placing a 1, 2 or 3 by the A tasks. Those identified as A-1 would be tackled first.

Yet another method (and my personal favorite) is to review the list with this question in mind: "What three or four things must I accomplish today in order to feel that my time has been worthwhile?" This less scientific, more mystical approach plays off the premise that we intrinsically know what our priorities should be, we just need a little push to face them. If on a given day the mind just won't work this way, one of the other prioritizing techniques can be applied.

Regardless of the method, finding a way to establish priorities should be on the top of every life manager's list.

High Priority Guidelines

There are a few guidelines that govern the setting of priorities.

Ideally, priorities should be about what's important, not what's urgent. It's easy to fall into the trap of putting situations that come up on the spur of the moment on top of the list. While the need to address such items is very real, these are not to be considered the day's priorities. Actually they are merely distractions from priorities. This supports the need to have only three or four top tier tasks to accomplish each day. It also underscores the importance of setting those priorities early in the morning or the previous evening, before urgent matters come up. Once the distraction is cleared, efforts should go back to what's really important.

Priorities are, and should be, heavily influenced by environment. This means that during a vacation, work-related items need not show up on the day's short list. Likewise, a serious in-depth telephone call with your financial planner may not make sense as a priority while you're taking care of newborn triplets. Again, some pre-planning is required for optimum effectiveness, this time possibly much further in advance. If you know you'll be going on a motorcycle road trip in a few days, handle your priorities that require writing e-mail before getting on the bike.

A span of several days' priorities should reflect a good balance of all the important roles of life. It's not healthy to focus only on career pursuits for days on end. Likewise, just having fun and not making progress professionally, or ignoring one's health over an extended period are recipes for disaster.

Setting priorities is a necessary part of effective living, simply because of the volume of items that are in our courts. Mastering this part of life management will make us far more fulfilled than facing our days in a haphazard manner. And almost nothing is more important than that.

I think a hero is an ordinary individual who finds the strength to persevere and endure in spite of overwhelming obstacles.
- Christopher Reeve

Have you ever wanted to be considered a hero? Maybe you thought you weren't made of the right stuff. But consider this: everyone we call a hero was known as just an ordinary person before encountering the circumstances that revealed the courage within.

True heroes don't spend their days looking for ways to take center stage. They simply live, applying their core beliefs and principles. They display integrity and refuse to compromise.

Most likely, your life presents difficult situations regularly. You draw on your resources and strength of character to overcome them. Should the challenges reach a greater level, including one that's nearly impossible, you will no doubt conquer those as well. The hero was there – inside you – all along.

Baby Steps For Big Results

A list of prioritized next steps toward accomplishing goals is a wonderful tool. But nothing happens until we actually do something. That part of the life management process can be called "execution."

To execute effectively, you must proceed in the way that works best for you. Otherwise, you either won't be challenged or you'll burn out.

The beginning piano student can't practice complex classical pieces for ten hours a day like the professional concert pianist does. He or she will get discouraged and give up. So the student plays more simple pieces for half an hour at a time. Someone who wants to lose a few pounds is more likely to be successful by cutting out one bad habit a month than by vowing to live on lettuce and grapefruit starting tomorrow. Those short term goals eventually add up, and real progress results.

True gains are made, not in huge leaps, but in tiny steps. That's how plans are successfully executed.

Elements Of Execution

The concept of execution is so simple that it's difficult to describe. In the title of a book by Larry Bossidy and Ram Charan, it's defined as "The Disciple Of Getting Things Done." That says it all.

Discipline is certainly important. Outside forces and inner voices try to distract us. These must be postponed, ignored, or at least handled swiftly. Then it's back to the matter at hand.

Sheer willpower, however, is not enough to sustain execution. A clear vision of the final outcome is needed. Working out at the gym for its own sake is often abandoned before long. But if the same person can get a picture in his mind of a time when he is lean, trim, muscular, and a great specimen of health for his age, it gives the activity deeper meaning and chances for success.

Adding emotion is exponentially helpful as well. Thinking of how pleased she will be when she looks in the mirror at some future date, or how proud her husband and children will be of her can go a long way toward helping a woman stay on a diet and exercise regime. Many a former couch potato has been able to finish a marathon by visualizing the thrill of crossing the finish line. When the reality comes, tears of joy follow.

Perhaps the most serious enemy to execution is procrastination. Failure is far more often accompanied with "I'll do it tomorrow" than by "I no longer want to do it." At the root of most procrastination is some aspect of fear – fear of the unknown, of failure, or even of success. An extremely helpful technique is to ask "What am I fearing?" Then write the answer on paper and look at it. Fears almost always lose their power when exposed to such light.

Execute. Do it. Get it done. There's no substitute.

Next Step?

Here's a tip that will help you perform to a higher degree of your potential in all areas of life.

Whenever you are working on a project, ask yourself "What is the next step that needs to be taken after the step I'm doing now?"

Sometimes you will find that the next step has to be accomplished by someone other than yourself. In that case, you are done with your part of the project (at least for the moment). But in many cases, you will find that there is a next step that you can do.

For example, let's say you are looking at a word in a draft of a business proposal, and you think the word looks odd. It crosses your mind that it may be misspelled. What will you do? You could do nothing, bring it to someone else's attention, or ask yourself "What is the next step?"

Most likely, the next step is to look the word up in the dictionary, or type it in to a good spell checker. Then, after determining that the word is indeed misspelled, you can take that information to whomever is responsible for the document and say, "I thought this word looked odd, so I looked it up in the dictionary, and sure enough, it is misspelled." No doubt, the latter is the better of the three options.

There are many examples of taking the next step, and of not taking the next step, that happen every day. In fact, as I was thinking about this concept, I asked myself "What should be the next step in sharing this with others?" The fact that you're reading it tells you the step I took.

Either I will find a way, or I will make one.

- Sir P. Sidney

Sometimes the path from where we are to where we want to be is clear. In those moments we simply follow the course set before us. Often, however, the road to accomplishment of our goals must first be constructed before it can be travelled.

To be successful requires innovation. The greatest strides in business, relationships, charitable work, the arts, etc., have come from those who broke new ground. While others were playing it safe, these people ventured into unexplored territory.

It is one thing to play a great symphony – quite another to write one. If the symphony of your life has not yet been written, put your creativity to work and compose it yourself. One day you may receive the standing ovation you deserve.

Another To Do List? Not.

Jim Collins, author of *Good To Great*, studied companies that achieved and sustained extraordinary success. Then he found common traits among them. Here is one of Collins' observations, as recorded in an interview in *Business Week* magazine:

"As I look at the most effective people we've studied, a 'stop-doing' list or 'not-to-do' list is more important than a to-do list, because the to-do list is infinite."

A Not-To-Do list. Amazing! What a concept!

What could it mean to your life and mine if we made a list of what not to do, and then stuck to it? Have you ever committed to something and later wished you hadn't? You could put it on your Not-To-Do list for future reference.

Have you noticed a time-wasting, dreaded, or even harmful habit or activity in your life? Maybe that should go on the Not-To-Do list, as well. This mindset can be fruitful on both business and personal levels.

After many years of navigating lengthy, multiple To-Do lists, I've seen how this new way of thinking positively affects my life. But I've got to stop writing now. I've got a whole bunch of stuff not to do.

Graduation Day Lessons

Graduation Day. A time when determination, sacrifice and hard work give way to celebration and the passage from classroom to career. For graduating students, the big day reflects the life management process in many ways.

First, these students identified a mission. There is something they hope to accomplish in life, so they chose a field of study. No doubt their missions line up with overall core values. And from the very beginning, they had a vision of life after school is done – a profession, their own apartment, etc.

Next came written goals. Each of the students had to know which classes to attend and when. They didn't just walk onto campus and wander into a classroom. Short term goals led to long term goals, all part of an overall plan with a timeline that was also in writing.

Along the way came the execution of prioritized tasks. Extra effort had to be given to writing a paper or studying for an exam, while other interests or pleasures were set aside. There's a price to pay to accomplish a goal.

It's likely that adjustments were made. Some students changed their major. Others may pursue a completely different field even after their education is done. There's nothing wrong with that – it's called reinventing yourself, and it's sometimes necessary.

While this is a very simplistic analysis, it points out the truth that getting to graduation day doesn't come by accident. It requires following a defined process.

Likewise, living a successful, effective, fulfilled life involves a systematic approach. That process is called life management. Those who follow its path accomplish much more in less time than those who don't. Like students charting their course for a brighter, more rewarding future, the benefits begin the day you enroll.

The greatest revelation of our generation is the discovery that human beings, by changing the inner attitudes of their minds, can change the outer aspects of their lives.

- William James

Difficult circumstances are a fact of life. None of us will escape some degree of hardship. Human beings do, however, have options for determining how they will mentally react to their hardships. Those options are called attitudes.

Negative attitudes make our problems seem even bigger than they are. As we dwell on the obstacle, we may wind up feeling overwhelmed and helpless. Such thinking can take our minds to a place where coming up with a solution is nearly impossible.

Positive attitudes, on the other hand, are solution oriented. They free us to be creative. To realize our resources. To discover opportunities in the midst of challenges and to feel better in the process.

Don't deny the reality of tough situations. Strive to overcome them. But be sure to work on your mental attitude as well, for it can be a powerful force in your favor.

Increasing The Com In Marcom

Business people sometimes use the phrase "marcom." It means "marketing communications." A great concept, but many companies drop the ball in the space between the two words.

I remember hearing a radio commercial for the grand opening of a sub shop in my neighborhood. I'd get a sub for one dollar just by mentioning the DJ's name. As fate would have it, I was driving past their location at that very moment, and I was hungry so what the heck. The young lady behind the counter knew nothing about the promotion, and looked at me like I was trying to pull a fast one. She also told me there was no way to handle that in the computerized cash register. Of course the manager wasn't in, so I politely insisted she call him. Problem solved.

Or how about this? You see or hear an ad that says "Order online today and get free shipping." But when you go to the web site, the shipping charge shows up no matter what you do.

The breakdown that occurred in both cases is a simple one. Important information never made it to the front lines.

Business involves communication – with the outside world, yes, and also with internal departments of the company. Imagine how much greater the impact of the sub shop promo would have been had the in-store staff said "Great. I see you heard our radio spot. Why not get a second sub and take it home to your wife? It's only a dollar." Sure, they were losing money on every sale, but the good will and excitement they could have generated might have made us long-term, repeat customers.

Marcom is important to an organization, and should always come with a hefty dose of com.

Do You Dare To Market?

A few years ago I met with the owner of a commercial landscaping company. His business had several crews taking care of the grounds of condominium complexes and the like. They were true professionals, did great work, and were considering me as their marketing consultant.

"Why would a property manager hire your company instead of one of your competitors?" I asked. His reply was "We're committed to customer satisfaction. If our customer isn't happy, we'll bring the whole team back, and re-do anything they want."

"Brilliant!" I said. "There's your marketing message." Let's make that the first thing people see on your web site and every piece of company literature. The approach will be: "If you're not thrilled with our work, call within 48 hours. We'll make it right – no charge."

"Are you crazy?" the prospective client exclaimed. "People will take advantage. Our scheduling will be all out of whack. Our dispatchers won't know how to prioritize. We can't do that."

That incident, and a few others like it that I've had in my career, point out one reason why some promotional efforts just don't work.

Sure, companies can play safe. They can use bland slogans and headlines like "Quality. Integrity. Service." But mediocre messaging returns mediocre results.

When FedEx declared that they'd take care of my package when it "Absolutely, positively has to be there overnight," it got my attention. The contractor who promises "We'll be there within a one-hour window or you don't pay" makes me say "Wow." Are there risks involved with such claims? You bet.

Effective marketing takes guts. It also requires commitment from every department in the company – not just the ad people. The upside far outweighs the downside, however. So be bold, prepare properly throughout the organization, and then get ready to take the orders.

Strategic And Tactical, The One-Two Punch

The proper combination of strategies and tactics can be extremely productive. Here are a few thoughts that will help in an understanding of each.

- Strategic thinking sets the goals.
- Tactical thinking determines how to achieve the goals.

- Strategic thinking focuses on the end which can be accomplished by the means.
- Tactical thinking focuses on the means which will be used to accomplish the end.

- Strategic thinking draws the road map.
- Tactical thinking gets the car down the road.

- Strategic thinking looks as far into the future as possible.
- Tactical thinking gets things done as quickly as possible.

- Strategic thinking plans ahead.
- Tactical thinking makes the best use of right now.

- Strategic thinking expands the possibilities.
- Tactical thinking narrows the variables.

- Strategic thinking pays little attention to obstacles, problems, what-ifs, etc. that could hinder the strategies.
- Tactical thinking confronts the obstacles and overcomes them.

- Strategic thinking is not concerned with time constraints.
- Tactical thinking is concerned with day to day, or even minute by minute, actions.

- Strategic thinking provides leadership.
- Tactical thinking provides management.

- Strategic thinking focuses on doing the right things.
- Tactical thinking focuses on doing things right.

- Strategic thinking decides which hill to take and gives the order to "Take that hill."
- Tactical thinking decides how to take the hill and then takes it.

- Strategists decide what to do.
- Tacticians get it done.

Which is better? Neither ... and both. A healthy mix of strategies and tactics, applied at the right times, is essential in any organization or individual life.

People Power

It takes a great many resources to operate a business. Computers, printers, desks ... all are necessary. Even paper, pens and rubber bands fill vital roles.

But what are the most important resources in any workplace? People. Nothing is of greater value.

You take care of the equipment used in your job and wouldn't think of harming any of it. Upgrading it when possible is preferred. That same thinking must be applied to co-workers. Is there something you can do to help them improve as individuals or professionals? And what can you learn from someone on the team?

Take initiative to make the people around you even better and let them do the same for you. You'll be improving the most important part of the organization.

Anatomy Of An A-Player

People who perform to a high degree of their potential are often called A-Players. Here are a few of their characteristics.

A-Players are lifelong learners. Experts say that if you read 30 minutes a day about your field, you will be in the top 5% of that field within two years. At first this sounds far-fetched. But if you think about how few people read anything, let alone 30 minutes a day, it becomes believable. A colleague of mine seems to always be up to speed on the latest developments. Recently I asked him "How did you know that?" He replied, "I read things."

A-Players go the extra mile. To be among the top people in your industry, you have to sometimes come in early, stay late, and find ways to be more productive. There's always room for improvement.

A-Players bring solutions, not problems, to a situation. Instead of saying "I don't know," the A-Player says "I'll find out." Instead of "It can't be done," it's "I'll figure out a way to do it." Being presented with a solution feels like a breath of fresh air to a customer – or to a boss.

No doubt there are many more characteristics of A-Players. These few, however, will take you a long way in that direction.

Stacking The Lineup With Stars

A-Players are star performers, those who go the extra mile to be at the peak of their professions. But how do they fit into a winning team that can make a company unbeatable?

In order to have a top team, you must have several different types of A-Players. Depending on your industry and organizational structure, you may need A-Players in sales, customer service, research and development, information technology, human resources, and more.

Top leaders view every role as a starring role. They commit themselves to defining the needs, then filling them with the best people possible who will work together as a team.

A group of A-Players devoting their efforts toward a common objective is one of the most powerful forces on Earth. A company headed in that direction will always have the competitive edge.

Your Co-Worker, Your Customer

An internal customer is a person inside a company who interacts with the other employees of that same organization. They are bosses, subordinates, and fellow staff who often depend upon one another in order to do their jobs. They assign work, ask for help with projects, request advice or opinions, etc. Top notch organizations understand their importance. The benchmark is for every team member to treat internal customers as well as they treat the firm's external customers.

You know how to treat external customers, and how you like to be treated when you are the customer of a business. Internal customers deserve the same. Be enthusiastic, cooperative, helpful, and always eager to serve internal customers with a positive attitude.

When everyone on the payroll has the same overall goals and objectives, this becomes much easier. I then realize that those other people are not distractions or forces taking me away from my own tasks. Instead, they are an integral part of the success of the enterprise, which has a direct affect on my own well being in the long run. Helping them ultimately helps us all – including myself. And no doubt I'll be calling on someone for assistance in the future, making me his or her internal customer.

Strive to take care of external customers with excellence. Remember internal customers as well, and give them the service they deserve too. The result will be rewarding long-term relationships at every level.

Keep away from people who try to belittle your ambitions. Small people always do that, but the really great make you feel that you, too, can become great.

- Mark Twain

The company we keep has a significant impact on our personal growth. This is especially true when it comes to revealing our dreams. Some people make us feel that our goals are silly and will never be realized. Others inspire us to accomplish our objectives and even go beyond them.

One measure of a person's greatness is the degree to which he or she motivates others to higher levels. This truth is also a challenge, for each of us has the option to belittle or encourage those with whom we come in contact.

It is impossible to isolate ourselves from negative individuals. We can, however, be selective about with whom we share our ambitions. What's more, we can be an important source of inspiration to those around us ... and when we are, we have truly become great.

Important Questions

Asking two questions will have a huge positive effect on your ability to effectively complete a task or project. The questions are: "Why?" and "What's the purpose?"

Here are some examples:

When creating a brochure for a business, the people working on it should ask: Why am I writing or designing this? What is the purpose of this? Do I want to elicit a certain feeling from the reader? Simply inform? Get the reader to do something? Is there a particular message or product that needs to be emphasized or made most prominent?

Imagine the job of stuffing and sealing envelopes. If you ask "Why am I doing this?" new light is shed on what could have been considered a mundane task. Some answers might be: "I'm doing this to make money for the company, so that we can all enjoy job security." Or "I'm doing this to communicate with our customers so they will know about a product that can make their lives better." These answers show that stuffing and sealing envelopes is really important!

"Why" can also be a labor reducer and a time saver. You might ask yourself "Why am I filing this paper?" and realize that it doesn't have to be filed at all – it can be thrown away. Likewise, "Why am I writing this memo, or making this phone call, etc."

There are lots of good reasons to ask these two important questions. And that's precisely why I wrote this.

The Good Side Of Job Dissatisfaction

Do you love your job? I hope you do.

Are you happy with your job? I hope you're not.

At first that might sound like a contradiction, but think about it and you'll see that loving your job and at the same time not being totally happy with it can take you a very long way toward greater success.

When people love their jobs, they look forward to coming to work. They are eager to get on with the day's tasks. They do their best to exceed customers' expectations, take the next step, and "Wow" the internal customer (their coworkers) as well.

When people who love their jobs are also not 100% happy with their jobs, they look ahead to the next challenge. They take on new and greater responsibilities, even if those responsibilities require additional training, outside reading, or stretching their abilities.

I hope you love your job. That is because I want everyone reading this to enjoy themselves every day of their lives. I also want your company to grow and prosper and that can only happen through a team of A-Players who come together every day with a passion for what they do.

But I hope you're not completely happy with your job. I hope there is some excitement in you as you think of ways your job can grow and expand – ways it can test your capacity and bring you to new heights. I hope you feel that you'll be happier with your job a year from now than you are with it today. (And a year from then, and a year from then ...)

I love my job, but I'm not 100% happy with it. How about you?

Best, Worst, And Always

"It was the best of times. It was the worst of times." Those are the famous words written by Charles Dickens to begin the book *A Tale of Two Cities* in 1859.

For anyone who's been in the business world awhile, these words illustrate a recurring experience. It seems as though there are both great opportunities and enormous threats most always. If at any given moment all the opportunities came through, the company would see incredible success. On the other hand, if all the threats manifested at once, it would be dealt a serious blow.

If the law of averages is any barometer, some – but not all – of the "worst of times" threats do take place, creating discouraging situations that have to be addressed. Likewise, some – but not all – of the "best of times" opportunities generally come to fruition. Those are indeed more exciting. Hopefully, more good than bad will happen, at least in the long term, allowing the business to grow.

Basically Overcoming Uncertainty

It's hard to follow the news without being challenged to feel down and at least a little scared. It seems that the media takes pleasure in reporting everything negative and forecasting worse. For what it's worth, here's a strategy for facing uncertainty: Focus on the basics.

Of course this means something different for each of us. It could mean staying in touch with customers and prospects, submitting proposals for expanded business, providing expert consulting support, or developing new products and services. And it will mean doing all of this on a better than average timetable, at reasonable prices, with a standard of excellence that makes customers say "Wow!", all the while watching costs.

Sounds like the same old boring stuff, right? And in a way it is. It's boring, but it pays off in the long run.

There are some things you can't control. It does no good to give those any more attention than you have to. Simply pray, ask for guidance, and proceed accordingly.

There are many things you can control. To those you must give enormous energy by focusing on the basics. That's how to prevail in challenging times.

Permission Or Forgiveness?

People sometimes pose the question, "Is it better to ask permission, or to take action and ask forgiveness?" The correct answer is "It depends." There are times when one or the other option is appropriate, and when they're not.

The debate over permission vs. forgiveness implies that differences exist in the values of those involved, such as friends, spouses, or a supervisor and his or her direct report. On the other hand, if everyone has the same objectives, the direction becomes more simple.

When all parties are working toward a common goal, none of them would intentionally do something that requires forgiveness. No one is perfect, however, so inadvertent errors occur. And when they do, the right course of action is to admit the mistake, humbly apologize, and take action to correct the problem. Unintentional errors should be the only times, therefore, that asking forgiveness is in order.

Situations in which a person lacks preparation and experience, that carry a significant downside, or with the possibility of serious consequences should trigger a request for permission. In a business setting, it's wise to go to someone higher in the organization. That person has probably been in similar positions before and knows what will likely work and what may not.

When a certain level of professional proficiency or relational familiarity has been achieved, and it's clear that the vision, strategies and goals are mutual, only then should one launch out on one's own. There will still be a level of risk present, as life comes with no guarantees, but the chance of success is much higher.

Asking permission is not a sign of weakness or immaturity, it's a characteristic of wisdom. And requesting forgiveness reveals humility and integrity more than failure. Both have their place in a life or company that is growing.

Procedures As Pillars

Michael Gerber is an author and the founder of Michael E. Gerber Companies, a business skills training firm based in Carlsbad, California. In his very popular books and seminars, he tells the story of the McDonald's breakfast that changed his life.

Michael Gerber was a salesman. One morning, he stopped at a McDonald's near his house for a breakfast sandwich on his way to his first appointment. Unfortunately, the prospect stood him up. So, to kill time before his next appointment, Michael stopped at another McDonald's across town. He was still hungry, so he ordered another breakfast sandwich.

It was then that Michael had an amazing realization ... the sandwiches were exactly the same. "How could this be," he asked himself, "since they are in two completely different restaurants, miles from each other, made by two completely different staffs of people?"

Gerber eventually discovered the secret to McDonald's consistency: Procedures. He found that this fast food chain has detailed procedures for every little thing they do. This, says Mr. Gerber, is why McDonald's can do extraordinary things with ordinary people. Or, as he tells his audiences, "McDonald's has built an empire using the same kids that you can't get to clean their rooms."

Procedures are the pillars of a well-run company. They provide a framework for people to grow as individuals and as a team.

Procedural Creativity

Systems. Procedures. Policies. A lot of people say "Yuck" when they hear those words. But policies and the like might not be so bad after all.

The systems, procedures, and policies at a well-run company are not designed to put people in a box or stifle creativity. Far from it. They are there for the purpose of building an efficient, organized operation. And believe it or not, an environment with systems, procedures, and policies actually promotes creativity.

For example, here is a procedure that is used at the advertising agency I lead: "Everything we work on, or everything we spend money on, must have a job number." Working on projects without job numbers would quickly become chaotic for the people in the agency. How would they name and archive digital files, keep track of bookkeeping, or log their time? How would they know how much to charge clients? The procedure, therefore, is a big help. But if anyone in the company wants to get creative and improve it, they're welcome to submit ideas.

When you read one of your company's policies or procedures don't view it as a static document carved in stone. Instead, think of it as a dynamic, changing document that was as good as it could be when it was developed, but which can be made even better.

Looking at policies, procedures, etc. in this way shows how these necessary elements of a company can actually inspire people to be creative.

Who Or What Is The Boss?

Who's the boss? Or in some cases, what's the boss? It's not always as simple as it seems.

A restaurant owner once taught that in his world there was no higher authority than the cash register. Every sale, he said, big or small had to go through that machine. Experience had shown him that once people started doing something as seemingly insignificant as making change out of their pockets, the business was on a very dangerous path.

In a service firm, the procedures manual may be king. It's a tool to keep the entire team going in the same direction, following processes that are proven to be profitable, and avoiding pitfalls. Deviate from the manual, and the organization can lose credibility while it chases its tail.

Who or what's the boss? Every business has to answer that question and make sure the whole team gets the message.

Procedures And An Old Car

Processes and procedures can keep an organization running smoothly. They help people stay on track and focused in both calm and chaotic times. Is it really that important, however, for a company to stick close to its procedures, or is good enough good enough? That question reminds me of one of my first cars, a 1973 AMC Hornet.

My AMC Hornet was great. It had nearly 200,000 miles on it when we separated. I loved driving it. But you might not have.

After a few years, the door hinges on the driver's side started to wear. To close the door I had to kind of lift up on it. Once I got used to that, though, it wasn't really a problem. Sometimes when I turned the windshield wiper knob, it came off in my hand. I adapted. The car pulled sharply to the right if I stepped hard on the brakes. Since I was aware, I made adjustments. And when I wanted to listen to the radio ... well, I just couldn't. The speakers rattled so badly that words or music were indistinguishable. So what? I carried a portable boom box on the passenger seat.

Yeah, the Hornet had idiosyncrasies. But they happened one at a time, over a period of years. And when something came up, I learned to live with it. It was no problem – unless someone other than me needed to drive the car. Then I had to explain everything. I have to admit, at those times I saw my Hornet as less than a luxury vehicle. In fact, it seemed more like a piece of junk.

The same principle can be true in business. Most firms start out with systems, procedures, and policies that cover everything from when the team is due to arrive in the morning to how they check out at night. In between, there are systems for the important aspects of the operation, who to consult for certain issues, what to do in an emergency, and much more.

If one person slacks off on one system, procedure, or policy, it might not seem like a big deal. The organization can adjust, just like I adjusted to the door hinges on my Hornet. But if those systems continue to be compromised and the company continues to adapt to the compromises, the day will come when the whole enterprise is in shambles.

You wouldn't have enjoyed driving my 1973 AMC Hornet. It had too many weird little quirks. But I hope you enjoy being part of the company you serve each day. Respecting its policies and procedures will help.

Tribute To The Blank Slate

There's something a bit unusual hanging on one of the walls in my office. It's a blank piece of paper, framed.

Every project starts with a blank slate. Whether it be paper or a computer screen, when you and I begin just about any endeavor there is nothing there. We have to make something happen. We have to design the ad, write the proposal, compose the budget, craft the strategy. Very often, the first step consists of staring at a blank screen.

Looking intently at a sheet of white can be hard work. The task seems overwhelming. But we jump in and start putting words, shapes or images on that page. We exercise discipline. Then, after time and a lot of effort, we have a finished product, or at least a first draft. The same holds true in the personal realm. Inspiring artwork, beautiful music, great literature – all began with nothing but a blank page.

Once transformed, those sheets that once held nothing touch millions of lives. Individuals and companies are willing to pay good money, express deep emotion, or commit their lives to a cause because talented people turned blank screens into other things.

I display that "picture" proudly. It is a tribute to everyone who has ever stared at a blank sheet or a blank computer screen and contemplated how they were going to begin a project. No doubt that includes you.

Who's Responsible?

"Who's responsible" is a question that has been discussed ever since the first man and woman were created. It's existed throughout human history, and it's made its way into every industry, business, and relationship. The right answer helps people grow closer. The wrong reply takes them swiftly downhill.

Let's envision a scenario where a mistake shows up in an important document. Everyone makes mistakes ... that's understood. The bigger concern, however, is the reaction to the question "Who's responsible?" Was it the person who created the document, the one who proofed it, or maybe the last set of eyes to approve it?

The correct answer is simple. Who's responsible? Everyone involved should say "I am." The mistake itself is a lot less troubling than people assigning blame to someone other than themselves.

Top notch companies and strong relationships are comprised of responsible people. When those with integrity hear the question "Who's responsible?", they reply with the simple word: "Me."

FYI

General information. Data. It comes our way in a steady stream. Some of it is meant just to keep us in the loop and requires nothing except to say "Thanks." Other times, however, that information can be a responsibility trigger. We may ask ourselves if some action on our part would be appropriate. We could ponder the next step and see if it's within our sphere of responsibility. If we answer "Yes" to either of those questions, we then need to do something.

If we don't want to drop everything to give attention to the new data, we may say "I'll look into that later," or "I'll think about it when I get a chance." There's nothing wrong with those responses as long as we actually take the action we intended reasonably soon.

Imagine someone giving you general information about a new ice cream shop in town. It might be fine for you to just say "Thanks." If, however, you're the sales manager for an ice cream cone bakery, some effort on your part might be in order (in addition to saying "Thanks.")

Simple information can be a responsibility trigger. Let it prompt you to look for opportunities to take action.

Perfectly Responsible

It is sadly rare to find people who take responsibility when things go wrong. But those who do show us the positive impact it can have, even in adverse circumstances.

On June 2, 2010, Armando Galarraga of the Detroit Tigers was on his way to pitching a perfect game. A perfect game is when a pitcher faces only 27 batters during the entire nine innings, and none of them make it to first base, because the pitcher and his teammates get every batter out. This had happened only 20 times in Major League Baseball history before that night, or about once every 20,000 games.

In the bottom of the ninth inning with two outs, Galarraga had to retire only one more batter to record a perfect game. The batter hit a ground ball, the throw beat the runner to first base by half a step. But amazingly, the umpire, Jim Joyce, called the runner safe. The perfect game, and Armando Galarraga's place in history, was gone.

More amazing than the near-perfect game, however, and more astounding than the blown call, was the umpire's response. Here are a few of the comments Jim Joyce made later that night in an interview with the press ... "I just cost that kid a perfect game." "No, I did not get the call correct." "It was probably the most important call of my career and I missed it."

Jim Joyce took responsibility.

The next night, the Detroit crowd gave Joyce a standing ovation. The Detroit Tigers team expressed their support for him. And two weeks later Jim Joyce was named the best umpire in baseball by a survey of Major League Baseball players themselves.

I wonder what players and fans would have thought if Jim Joyce had made excuses for his obvious mistake. Taking responsibility is powerful.

Responsibility And Authority

Responsibility is a two sided coin. On the flip side is authority. Stated another way, a person's authority is directly related to the amount of responsibility he or she has, and vice versa. Taking responsibility is a great way to grow in authority. Not taking responsibility is a clear indication that a person is not ready for more authority.

The person who wants more authority must also take responsibility. For someone in an administrative position, it might mean volunteering to head a new focus area or project. For a sales person, it might involve coming up with a more effective way to generate new business and sharing it as a best practice. Those who are given authority are typically the ones who first take added responsibility.

It starts with being responsible for one's designated position and assignments. Then when something above and beyond comes along, step up and take responsibility for that as well. Authority will certainly follow.

Why not upset the apple cart? If you don't, the apples will rot anyway.

- Frank A. Clark

We all have times when we wish things could stay exactly as they are. But, that can never be. Our observations, experiences, and even the laws of physics teach us that if we are not progressing, we are losing ground.

Since stagnation is equal to regression, let's avoid standing still at all costs. Pursue our dreams. Take calculated risks. Have some fun simply for the sake of having fun.

Carts full of perfectly stacked and polished apples can look nice, but sometimes they're just plain boring. And the apples underneath might be rotting away. Wouldn't it be great to upset that apple cart now and then?

The "Should I?" Question

All of us face situations where, at least for a moment, we don't know what to do. In those times, before asking someone "Do you want me to... ?", consider first asking yourself: "Should I...?"

For example, as part of my job I often handle printing assignments for clients, acting as the client's representative. Let's suppose I get a price quote from a printer and it seems too high.

I could call the client and say, "The price quote seems high, do you want me to get a second price quote?" Or I could first ask myself "Should I get a second price quote?" In this example, if the original price quote seems too high, I should get a second quote. It's the proper thing to do for the client.

Other examples:

You are given something to review. A document contains an obvious misspelling:
Before asking someone: "Do you want me to correct that word?"
Ask yourself "Should I correct that word?"

A courier service is late picking up a package:
Before asking someone: "Do you want me to call the courier service and see why they're late?"
Ask yourself: "Should I call the courier service and see why they're late?"

There will be times when you honestly don't know if you "should." In those cases, you will ask yourself the "Should I" question and you will answer that question "I don't know if I should." You can then feel free to ask someone the "Do you want me to" question.

The key is to ask yourself the "Should I" question first.

What Do You See?

One thing that a person who wants to be more responsible can do is to purposely, mindfully look – visually – for specific opportunities to take responsibility within his / her surroundings. Think of these as visual responsibility triggers.

This can mean viewing a work space more carefully to notice improvements that can be made. For example, pause outside your office and tell yourself that when you open the door you are going to try to see things through the eyes of someone who is visiting for the first time.

It could be approaching a project that's already finished, then taking a deep breath and asking "What can I find in this that can be made better?"

Or it might mean deliberately perusing the common areas of the shop as you walk from one spot to another, trying to see papers and items out of place, or something that needs to be straightened or cleaned.

In the book *Selling Retail*, author John Lawhon tells about a furniture store manager who tried to keep the displays looking perfect. Yet when the District Supervisor stopped in, he always found specs of dust on the furniture. One day the manager asked the supervisor how he was able to do that. The supervisor replied "When I walk through your store, I am only looking for specs of dust."

Learning to truly see is a matter of conscious, intentional focus. As Yogi Berra said, "You can observe a lot just by watching." Visual responsibility triggers are literally all around us.

Taking Responsibility

People talk about taking responsibility. It's a wonderful concept. What's more, a quick analysis of that phrase itself can reveal some important truths.

"Taking" is an action word, a verb. In order, therefore, to take responsibility, we have to actually do something.

Opportunities to take responsibility abound. The need can be triggered by things we see, by information and data that comes into our orbit, by asking ourselves questions, by requests from co-workers, family and friends, and in many other ways. When faced with one of these triggers, a decision is in order.

Choosing to do nothing leads to personal failure. Sometimes we have to respectfully decline. If the matter is outside my area of responsibility, it's better that I say "No" and save my capacity for something else. In other cases, I can defer my efforts until it's more convenient. I must be diligent, however, not to let my rightful duties fall through the cracks and into a black hole. When appropriate, the proper response will result in an action.

When faced with such situations, the next step is completely up to me. Responsibility will not force itself into my court. I have to reach out, grab it, and perform. That's called taking responsibility.

Victim Mentality

The opposite of approaching life as a responsibility-taker is to have a victim mentality. This self-limiting mindset can show itself in many ways. Here are a few examples of situations viewed through two very different sets of eyes:

Victim Mentality – The clerk at the store sold me the wrong item.
Responsibility-Taker – I bought the wrong item.

Victim Mentality – The supplier never got back to me with a price, so we lost the deal.
Healthy Responsibility – I didn't follow up with the supplier, so we lost the deal.

Victim Mentality – I missed the call because my phone's battery was dead.
Responsibility-Taker – I missed the call because I forgot to charge my phone's battery.

Being aware of these distinctions is extremely important. That's because a victim is powerless, helpless, and cannot make the situation better. He or she is stuck and that's that. Bad stuff will just keep happening and nothing can be done about it. A person who takes responsibility, on the other hand, knows that there are actions s/he can take to make the current situation better and to avoid negative outcomes in the future.

If the reason I missed a call is because the phone's battery was dead and nothing more, that's the end of the story. Phones don't ring when their batteries are dead, and I can't be expected to answer a phone that doesn't ring. But if the reason I missed a call was that I forgot to charge the battery, then there are ways I can improve the situation in the future. I can charge the battery overnight. If I have a hard time remembering, I can put the charger on my night stand, or put a note on the mirror where I brush my teeth before bed, or buy an extra battery if overnight charging isn't enough, or … There are a number of steps to try if I'm willing to take responsibility.

People with victim mentality should not be placed in high positions in an organization. When the leader is bent in that direction, the whole culture will go there.

If you think of yourself as a victim, life becomes an unbeatable enemy. Much better in every way is to identify those areas where you have control, then take responsibility and emerge victorious.

It's All About Responsibility

Responsibility is a big word with a major influence on the success of individuals and organizations.

When things go wrong and you're involved, the primary question to ask is "Who's responsible?" and the best answer to that question is "I am." Sidestepping issues, assigning blame for mistakes, avoiding the hard stuff, displaying a victim mentality, etc. are sure signs of lack of responsibility. Saying "I'm responsible" shows a sincere desire to grow.

On the flip side of responsibility is authority. A person's scope of authority is directly related to the amount of responsibility that person is willing to shoulder, and vice versa. Management that assigns responsibility without granting authority is poor management. Likewise, team members who refuse to take responsibility will not get far down the road to greater authority.

There are a few things that cross our paths that can function as responsibility triggers. These are words, phrases, and situations that prompt our minds to consider taking responsibility at that moment. A few of them are:

- The "Should I" question. This means that before you ask someone else "Do you want me to … ?" you ask yourself "Should I … ?"

- Thinking of the next step. This responsibility trigger occurs when we ponder what has to be done with a project or task after the part we're doing right now. Maybe it's something for which we can take responsibility.

- Visual responsibility triggers. Consciously learning to observe what's around us. Looking for opportunities to be responsible.

Like all good habits, taking responsibility can become something we train ourselves to do as we seek to have a positive impact in our daily lives.

I'll Find Out

When faced with a new challenge outside your comfort zone, and asked if it can be done, there are several possible replies.

The easy answer is "No, it can't be done." After a person answers "No" and walks away, that person can go back to whatever he or she was doing and not give the new challenge another thought. This is certainly not the type of person who grows and develops throughout life.

Another possible answer is "I don't know." This answer is better than "No" but still, the person who says "I don't know" takes no responsibility for the new challenge. Any future efforts are out of his or her hands.

A far better answer is: "I don't know, but I'll find out."

The "I don't know" part was honest. A person with this response isn't trying to pull the wool over anyone's eyes. That's good, because when people act as though they know something when they don't, they usually wind up over promising and under delivering which has negative consequences.

Then, after admitting "I don't know," saying "but I'll find out" is accepting the responsibility to find a solution. By adding that phrase, the person becomes a solution provider, rather than a source of another problem.

Great things happen to those who see challenges as opportunities to learn rather than taking the easy way out.

Accepting Our Imperfection

Nobody likes to make mistakes. That's especially true of people who have perfectionist traits and take their work very seriously. These are wonderful qualities, but when they become distorted, it can lead to a very uncomfortable and unproductive condition.

What's your number one thought when a mistake is uncovered? Do you immediately wonder if it was your fault, or do you first think of how the situation can be corrected? Do you attempt to prove that you did everything right, or do you forego that – at least for the time being – and make the necessary modifications? Do you primarily justify, or do you take responsibility and apologize? And when the dust settles, do you build a case for why you couldn't have been expected to do anything differently, or do you look for ways to change your process and avoid the error next time, then commit to that new course of action?

While self-preservation is human nature, it's clear which answers are more beneficial. It's important to focus on solutions, improvements, and raising the bar – even if it means admitting our own shortcomings.

Everyone is imperfect. That's not a problem. Extremely dangerous, however, are imperfect people who try to convince others that they're perfect.

Collaborate with reasonable, honest people who care about creating the best output possible. When they sometimes miss the mark, they'll handle the situation appropriately and get even better.

From Unwise To Wise

People who want others to think they are never wrong are scary. Inside their excuses, reasons, explanations, finger-pointing and the like, is something additional. There's a person in there who's lost the ability to learn ... who is not moving forward in life.

A student once asked his mentor "How did you learn to make wise decisions?" The mentor replied: "Through experience." The student questioned: "How did you gain experience?" The mentor answered: "Through decisions that were unwise."

Un-wisdom leads to wisdom. Mistakes lead to knowledge. Being wrong leads to learning new lessons and moving forward. But pretending to be perfect and trying to cover up shortcomings only creates a stagnant existence.

If you think you already know everything, you'll never learn anything.

Danger! Perfectionist Ahead.

Inside many successful businesses, there's a high percentage of people who are perfectionists. On the surface, that's very good. Taken to a distorted extreme, however, it can be quite detrimental.

Let's start at the ending. What would it look like if we were part of a corporate culture that reflected the right attitude toward perfectionism? Here are a few thoughts ...

- When mistakes or areas that can be improved came to light, we would never hear phrases like "That's because ..." and "Well I thought you said ..." and "I must have gotten distracted by ..." and "He / She told me to ..." etc. A simple "Thank you for pointing that out" is often far better.

- We'd laugh at ourselves a bit more.

- We'd be more accepting of one another.

- We'd apologize for our oversights, commit to improving ourselves, and get even better.

- We'd take ourselves a little less seriously, and take the shortcomings more seriously.

- We'd save a lot of energy.

It's unrealistic to expect the perfectionist tendencies of those in a successful team to go away. Those traits are too ingrained and are, in many ways, admirable. The goal is to make the high standards part of a personal commitment to continually learn, improve, and grow.

I Was Wrong

There are three words in the English language that are extremely hard to pronounce. In fact, they are so difficult to articulate that very few people ever even attempt to say them. What are those three words? "I was wrong."

Admitting to being wrong isn't easy for anyone. But simply acknowledging an error and moving forward properly can do wonders for relationships. It can also reduce stress levels, cement good reputations, and help us find solutions while avoiding similar mistakes in the future.

There's an art to saying you're wrong. Those who master it will enjoy life all the more.

The first step is simple admission. Just "I was wrong." No excuses. No "but" statements. No explanations. Say "I was wrong" and nothing more.

The next step is looking toward the future, instead of looking toward the past.

During those times when people do admit they're wrong, they often follow it up with a view to the past. It goes like this: "I reacted in anger. But my spouse provoked me." "I made a typo. I guess someone distracted me." "I didn't bring that mistake to anyone's attention because nobody told me to." These statements all look to the past.

How much better it is to look to the future. For example: "I reacted in anger. I will speak more calmly from now on." "I made a typo. I'll be sure to check my work better." "If ever I should notice a mistake again, I'll bring it to the right person's attention." These are solution-oriented statements that include a commitment for self improvement.

If people can admit their shortcomings, then look to the future instead of the past, it will greatly improve their professional and personal relationships. And I don't think I'm wrong about that.

Perfectionists Unite!

When a team of people is comprised of a high percentage of perfectionists, it sometimes creates challenges. But if they channel those qualities properly, the upside can be huge. Here are a few ways to put perfectionist tendencies to good use:

- Improve one another's work, enhancing the performance of the entire organization. This means showing others what you're doing, getting a second opinion, being humble enough to reach out for help, etc. Find ways to make the company and everyone in it – not just yourself – look good.

- Cover coworkers' backs. It's not a "gotcha" thing, it's a "help ya" thing. Awhile back, the finance manager at my company very kindly pointed out a typo that I made in a document. I was embarrassed, but grateful. She could have taken the position that this document was not her responsibility because it had nothing to do with finance. Instead, she made it her responsibility and the company benefited.

- Improve on the customer's input or request. At my advertising agency, we never put out sub-standard work because "That's what the client wants," or "That's what they sent me." Sometimes we may have to show clients what they requested, but we also show a second version that is, in our opinion, a better option.

It's good to be serious about wanting everything as near perfect as possible, as long as you focus that energy in the right direction.

Excuses Have A Downside

Excuses. Reasons. Rationalizations. People often want to explain any time they fall short. But excuses have a huge downside that can do far more harm than good.

Some rationalizations are valid. Being a no show at a meeting because the flight was delayed is different from getting to the airport late because I was absorbed in a video game. The first is a reason beyond my control. The second is an excuse that tells the world I have my priorities messed up. And a pattern of tardiness is a signal that life is running me and not vice versa.

So, if we miss the mark for some reasons, an explanation is acceptable, though if it happens too often, we might get a reputation for crying "Wolf." For situations within our control, it's best just to apologize, vow to do better, and move on.

Don't fall prey to the negative consequences of your own excuses.

Perfectly Imperfect

We've all heard the saying "If it's worth doing, it's worth doing perfectly." But how about this: "If it's worth doing, it's worth doing imperfectly – at first."

Many times we get bogged down, even sort of paralyzed by the desire for perfection. We stare at the computer screen trying to come up with brilliance; we gaze into the air waiting for the right idea. In those cases, often the best course of action is to simply make SOME move in the right direction. Do SOMEthing ... and then refine it later.

There are also situations when we spend far too much time getting one small part of a project just so. The list of tasks on our plate continues getting longer, but we neglect those and tweak the current project over and over even though it's just fine as is. When we are at last ready to declare completion, we feel empty, as if the extra efforts weren't really worth it (which they may not have been), and now we're backed up and overwhelmed besides.

I wish I had time to make this article the most well-written one ever. I don't. Perhaps one day I'll come back and edit it, but not now. I felt, however, that this concept was worth sharing ... so it was worth sharing imperfectly.

This Title Contained A Mistake

I have a confession to make. Here it is: I make a lot of mistakes. Tons, in fact. Almost every memo I write, spreadsheet I create, e-mail I compose, etc. has one or more mistakes in it.

My colleagues would likely disagree, having seen very few errors in my work over the years. Why is that? Because I almost always carefully check what I do before I let anyone other than myself see it. I won't say that I catch ALL my blunders, but I get most of them.

Mistakes cost companies a lot of money, and damage corporate and personal reputations as well. The first line of defense against that happening is to take a few extra minutes and check what you've done before releasing it. This must become a mandatory, second-nature part of a corporate culture. The goal should be for zero mistakes to see the light of day.

Most of us try hard to do everything perfectly. Knowing, however, that we'll never get there, it pays to check (and re-check) work before letting it go. When an error of any kind does slip past, forego the finger pointing and excuses and simply admit your humanness with a view toward improvement in the future.

And P.S. – If there are any typos in this book that got by my spell-check and proofreading, I take full responsibility. And I'll try to do better from now on.

When one person hesitates because he feels inferior, the other is busy making mistakes and becoming superior.

\- Henry C. Link

A mother was helping her son learn to ride a bicycle. For more than an hour, she ran alongside him, holding the bike while the boy strained to keep his balance. She was exhausted and ready to give up when an older brother said, "Mom, would you like me to help him?" The mother accepted gladly, went inside, and sat down to rest.

Barely ten minutes later, the older boy walked into the house. "I thought you were going to teach your brother to ride a bike," the mother said. To which her son replied, "I showed him how to fall without getting hurt. Now he'll be able to learn by himself."

How many opportunities have you and I missed because we were afraid to make a mistake? Instead, those very mistakes can be highly effective instructors, paving the way to success.

Some Assembly Required

Christmas Eve. The time when Santa begins making his way to every family that celebrates this holiday, leaving presents for boys and girls. Late that night or early the next morning, in homes all across the world, parents face those three words that bring fear to their hearts: Some Assembly Required.

Bicycles, swing sets, doll houses, wagons, stereos … they all come in pieces and have to be put together. Sometimes the result is a thing of beauty that looks exactly like the picture on the box. Often, however, there are skinned knuckles, arguments between spouses, and parts left over.

Business is similar. Profits don't magically pop out of the package. The successful company has to be assembled bit by bit. In an organization, there is rarely a detailed instruction manual or a photograph of the finished product to use as a guide. Someone has to envision the desired outcome in his or her mind.

Our personal lives require some assembly as well. Life management, physical exercise, mental stimulation, spiritual growth, and individual development are all critical to reaching our full potential.

Some assembly is definitely required if anything useful is to come from a bunch of miscellaneous pieces. That's true in business, in life, and in the basement or garage at 2:00 A.M. on December 25 where Mom and Dad scratch their heads while the children listen for sleigh bells and try not to sleep.

The Two Hardest Parts – Number Two

There are two parts of any task or project that are the hardest of all. One of them is – Finishing It. (To find out what the other one is, see the first entry in this book.)

Bringing a task or project to completion can be difficult. This is a double-sided coin. On one hand, we may lose momentum when the end is in sight and the excitement begins to wane. An equally deadly trap is to feel that we can do just one more thing to make the effort better.

Starting a project, once we get over our own inertia, can be euphoric. So much opportunity lies ahead! As time goes on, however, and the grind of working hard at it becomes reality, that initial high can subside. Strangely, it's not uncommon to lose interest when the finish line is in sight. How many paintings sit in closets, garages, and attics for lack of a few final strokes?

For many people, the closer they get to the goal, the more new details, ideas, and challenges arise. This may be a self induced symptom of perfectionism, masked as the feeling that the outcome could be just a little bit better if only ... There's even some deceptive truth to this dilemma. But unless you're a surgeon or an airline pilot, getting to 100% perfection is usually not necessary. When incremental improvements become miniscule, it's time to say "Enough" and declare completion.

One technique for mastering these hurdles is to visualize the joy and fulfillment that will come when the item is truly behind you. There's nothing quite like the word "Done" or a big, thick cross off on the to-do list. Another method is to plan a personal reward when all the open loops can be closed. And don't cheat yourself. Make sure to take and enjoy the prize, no matter how big or small.

Finishing a task or project is not easy, but it is possible. And with that, this book is complete.

Steve Fales is available for public speaking, individual coaching, and organizational consulting. For information and additional articles similar to the ones in this book, visit the author's website/blog: www.twentythousandfeet.com.

Epilogue

If the concepts in this book have helped your life in any way, the greatest joy you can give this author is to live in harmony with those and pass them along to people you know.

> *And what you have heard from me,*
> *commit to faithful men and women*
> *who will be able to teach others also.*

About The Author

Steve Fales describes himself as an ordinary guy with an intense drive to have a positive effect on everyone he meets. He and Linda, his wife of more than three decades, live in south Florida and enjoy staying abreast of the adventures of their two grown daughters.

Steve is the founder of several businesses, including an advertising/marketing agency with national clients. He maintains a rigorous physical training schedule in support of endeavors as an endurance runner and triathlete. Through writing, presentations, and coaching, he communicates techniques and principles for personal and professional development and biblical spiritual growth.

Steve's life mission is to leave a legacy of having achieved his full potential and helping others do the same.